50 CREA

Dedication

I want to dedicate this book to my best friend, my husband Ray. Ray is the best ideas person I have ever known and most of the ideas in this book originally came through him. He has a unique gift of being able to think of masses of fresh, inspiring ideas but is constantly reaching out to God so that his ideas have the prophetic hand of God on them.

50 Creative Worship Ideas

NANCY GOUDIE

EASTBOURNE

ISBN 1 84291 027 2

Published by
KINGSWAY COMMUNICATIONS LTD
Lottbridge Drove, Eastbourne, BN23 6NT, England.
Email: books@kingsway.co.uk

Book design and production for the publishers by
Bookprint Creative Services, P.O. Box 827, BN21 3YJ, England.
Printed in Great Britain.

Contents

SMELL

HEARING

SIGHT

IMAGINATION AND FAITH

Acknowledgements

I would like to thank the following people for their help while I was writing this book.

To June, my personal assistant, for the help you gave me when I needed to do some research for this book. Thank you, June. I really enjoy working with you.

To my admin support team, Ally, Zoe, Suse and June. You have been such a great encouragement and support to me – thank you all.

To Dave Roberts, Carolyn Owen and all at Kingsway. It's been a joy to work with you.

To my husband, Ray, and my sons Daniel and Aidan. I could not have written this book without your help and prayers. I love you all so much.

A special thanks to Ray for your constant love and encouragement and for your 'ideas' throughout the years. As I said earlier, most of the ideas in this book have come through you and the unique gift God has given you.

To all my intercessors, for your constant prayer support. I value each of you so much.

To my incredibly faithful heavenly Dad through whom all great 'ideas' have their birth. What can I say? Without you I would not exist, never mind this book.

Introduction

Where did you get such a brilliant idea?

Just recently, my husband Ray celebrated a very special birthday: he reached the BIG FIVE O! As his birthday drew closer, I was extremely concerned that I would not be able to think of a present that seemed 'special' enough for him. So I thought I would consult the greatest creative mind in the universe – my heavenly Dad! While praying and asking God what to do, I felt God give me a great idea. Whether I had heard this idea previously from someone and God brought it to my mind I don't know, but I decided that I would give Ray a present every month throughout the year to make his whole year special. I bought twelve cards and on each card I wrote what his present was for that month. Some months the presents were big, like a romantic trip to Paris, and other months the presents were smaller, like breakfast in bed. Some presents were trips I had arranged to see special friends whom we hadn't seen for many years because of the pressure of our work. All the presents were thought through carefully with Ray in mind. I picked presents that I knew he would love.

As I wrapped up his 'present', I was desperately hoping that I had heard God correctly. The present didn't seem very much – only twelve little cards – but so much thought, work and prayer had gone into it. The morning of his birthday arrived and although I, and our boys Daniel and Aidan, had bought him a couple of other presents, it didn't look as though it was a present fit for a special birthday. I handed Ray his carefully wrapped cards and said, 'This is your main present. I really hope you like it.' As he looked at it very curiously, I was anxiously thinking, 'Oh, maybe I should have bought something else.' However, when he opened it I was totally unprepared for his reaction. As he opened each card and read what it said, he was visibly moved and tears started coming to his eyes. When he finished, he told me it was the most special present he had ever received.

When Ray told others about his present, quite a number of friends said to their partners, 'What a great idea! Make sure you remember that one when it's time for me to celebrate a special birthday.' But I can't really take the credit for this great idea, because I know its inspiration came from God. Similarly this book is crammed with great ideas and although they came through me, Ray and others, the inspiration comes from the best creative mind in the universe: God! I am praying that as you use them, you will see God's creative hand in all you do.

Most of the ideas in this book have been ones that Ray and I have used throughout our years in full-time Christian work through Heartbeat and NGM. Some of them you might have seen in action if you have come to any NGM events or to my Spiritual Health conferences, which I hold each year in a four-star luxury hotel in Bristol. Some have originally come from others in or outside NGM, and where they have, I have tried to acknowledge that fact, but please do forgive me if I have inadvertently forgotten anyone's involvement.

One of the main differences in these ideas is that in each of them I have introduced the use of the senses God has given us. You cannot fail to notice that today we live in a very sense-conscious society. We are exhorted to 'feel the spirit', 'taste the excitement', or 'arouse the senses' through whatever product the advertisers are trying to sell. I feel it is so important in this sense-orientated culture that we explore, experience and use our God-given creativity. So often our worship and church meetings or events are one-dimensional, producing the feeling that they are in 'black and white'. These ideas are hopefully a way of bringing multidimensional creativity and colour in all its splendour back into our evangelism, worship and ministry. God has created us with five amazing senses, which give us the ability to see, touch, smell, hear and taste. In addition to this, he has made each of us with a keen imagination, which has been called the sense organ of the mind. In these ideas, I am simply encouraging us to use all this creativity within us to bring us into a deeper walk with God.

You will find that these ideas work just as well in small groups, such as cells or home groups, as they do in large audiences of perhaps hundreds of people. Some of the ideas are quick and will therefore complement what you are already doing in your meeting, whereas others will take longer.

When I was preparing Ray's gift, I had such fun thinking of all the presents he would like to receive and how I could make them extra special. It took a lot of time and effort, but the result was certainly worth it. I had to make phone calls and arrange flights, secret rendezvous, meals, etc. without him realising what I was doing, but the effort made the present special to Ray. Similarly, if we want our evangelism, church meetings and worship to be special, which I am sure each one of us does, then it will require us to make the time and the effort to reach out to God for what he would want us to do. My prayer is that through the use of this book these ideas will trigger you not only to experience God in new creative ways, but will also start you off on a new journey of reaching out to God and receiving fresh creative ideas for yourself.

Nancy Goudie

Taste

1 Come and Eat

THE PREPARATION

You will need to purchase a box of chocolates, making sure you have enough for one each for everyone present. They need to be individually wrapped, so Celebrations or Cadbury's Roses would be ideal. Place the chocolates on a plate so that people can choose their favourite sweet.

If you have an overhead projector or video screen, arrange to have the following verses displayed at the appropriate times:

* Isaiah 55:1–3
* Psalm 34:8

THE IDEA

Do not refer to this idea until the talk is about to start. Then, at the beginning of the talk pass the plate of chocolates around and encourage people to take their favourite one. Tell them not to open it but to put it on their notepad, Bible or knee, or somewhere where they will see it during the talk. Do not refer to it again until the very end of the talk.

At the end of the talk say something like, 'Many of you, when you picked your favourite chocolate from the plate, heard the "call" to eat this chocolate straight away. This chocolate was calling to you, "Come and eat!" The urge within you was strong and the message was clear. Just by looking at the chocolate you knew it was good, but you knew

17

that tasting it would be even better.' Then challenge people with the following: 'Have you heard the call of God today? God is calling you to greater intimacy. He is calling you to greater freedom. He is calling to you, "Come and eat."' Read Isaiah 55:1–3 (displayed, if possible, on the overhead or video screen).

'Is your response one of eagerness and hunger? You have heard the verse "Taste and see that the Lord is good", Psalm 34:8.' (Again, if you can, display the words of the verse as you quote it.) 'You knew just by looking at your favourite chocolate that eating it would be more than a pleasant experience. However, if you stopped at just looking, you would not have experienced all that your chocolate promised. God has promised that if you "taste" him, you will not be disappointed. Eat your chocolate, but also put your will into action and begin to experience a deeper taste of the Living God.'

I have used this idea with a large audience, but it would work perfectly with any number of people. One thing I should mention, don't be concerned about the cost of buying the chocolates. You will be surprised at how many chocolates there are in each box!

2 Come and Drink

This is an idea based on Psalm 34:8, which says, 'Taste and see that the Lord is good', inviting people to come and discover for themselves that God is indeed good and can affect their lives today. No matter what people are going through, this idea shows that God is sufficient for any need they have.

THE PREPARATION

Set out tables at various points in your venue. How many you need will depend on the size of your group. Place on the tables enough glasses for the number of people attending your event. You can usually borrow glasses from local supermarkets at no cost, as long as you book them in advance and return them the next day. You will, however, be asked to pay for any breakages. Purchase various bottles of water. Look for still, sparkling and all sorts of flavoured water, etc. Make sure you have more than you think you will need. (Supermarkets may allow you to purchase your bottles of water on a sale-or-return basis.) Make sure each bottle of water is chilled for the event. If you are not using the water until midway through your programme, then use cool bags, ice buckets or fridges to store them until needed.

Prepare someone to read John 4:1–26, 28–30, 39–42, making sure they have a good clear speaking voice and will rehearse the reading beforehand. This idea uses a meditation from my CD *A God Encounter*. You will find it on track 2. If you would prefer someone to read the meditation, again you will need someone with a clear voice but also someone who can read with expression and sensitivity. They need to be able to read the words in such a way that it will paint a picture in people's minds, so that they can 'see' what the meditation is saying. They can use the backing track 7.

Ask a couple of people to be prepared to give their story of how they met Jesus. Choose people who are clear about their faith and if necessary go through it with them beforehand.

Make sure you prepare your musicians, singers or worship leaders by going through the theme of the event with them. Ask them to sing and lead people in worship through songs that are complementary to the theme. As you pray beforehand with your team, it may be that God will give you words of knowledge or prophecies that would be appropriate to give out. Ask whoever received the word to be prepared, if it is appropriate in the event, to give the word out publicly.

Have several counsellors ready to pray for people who are 'thirsty' and in need of God in their lives. Ensure they are ready to pray for people who want to get to know Jesus for the first time. Have the counsellors stand at the tables at the appropriate time and ask people if they wish individual prayer when they come for a drink.

As your event is based on the theme 'Taste and see that the Lord is good', have the verse printed or painted on posters throughout the hall, or placed on a video screen.

You could have scenes of deserts or parched land on your overhead or video screen as people walk into the venue.

THE IDEA

Start the event by stating the theme. Explain that if people are feeling parched or drained of life, they have come to the right place. God is here and wants to bring his refreshment and his life.

Ask your appointed person to read John 4:1–26, 28–30,

39–42, and arrange, if possible, for the text to be put on the overhead or video screen at the same time. Then ask your appointed people to come and give their testimonies to God.

Next, use the following meditation. Ask people to sit or lie on the floor in a comfortable position, with their eyes closed. Ask them to concentrate on the words being spoken and to 'see' the picture being painted in their mind.

Water of Life

Close your eyes and in your imagination begin to see yourself in a very hot country. The place in which you find yourself is very bare and barren. The sun is shining brightly and the heat is unbearable. Feel the sun's hot rays on your body. It isn't long before your mouth is parched and you are longing for a long cool drink of water. A short distance away you see a well, but as you reach it you notice that this well has not been used for some time. There is no water and the bottom of the well is empty and dry. Disappointed, you turn away feeling even more thirsty and desperate.

As your eyes search the horizon, you see another well and with hope rising in your being you make your way towards it. With every step, your thirst drives your imagination to feel that long cool drink of water. On arriving, you are overwhelmed with relief and joy that this well is in order and is working. However, you discover that this well has a guardian. You approach the guardian and plead for some water. He replies, 'If you drink this water you will immediately be thirsty again, but I can give you special water – water that will satisfy your thirst and bring life and well-being to your body, mind and spirit.' You ask him where he can get water like that and he replies that the water comes from the fountain of life. He encourages you to taste and see and holds a cup of water to your lips. You take a sip and immediately you feel a huge difference as the water begins to penetrate your parched mouth. Your eyes begin to sparkle and it feels as if life is once more penetrating through your veins. You drink deeply this time, consuming all he has for you. With each drink you feel your body, mind and spirit being flooded with life and encouragement. This water is different – it is very thirst-quenching but also seems to bring lasting energy and leaves your body feeling alive and well, your mind energised and your inner being encouraged and fully satisfied.

You realise that instead of needing more water, it's as if you have a spring of water flowing from within you. The guardian was right about never being thirsty again. In fact you realise you have water within you to give away to others. You leave the well, eager to tell others about the special water you have received.

The Bible says, 'Come, all who are thirsty, come to the waters.' Reach out to God now and tell him you want more of him and his living water in your life. Jesus says to you, 'Drink deeply from the water I will give you and you will never thirst again.'

Nancy and Ray Goudie, Copyright © 2002

At the end of the meditation, at the appropriate point, invite people to go to the various tables and take a drink of the water. Tell them that there are various kinds of water, with all sorts of flavours, representing the fact that we have a God who is able to satisfy all sorts of needs. No matter who we are, God is able to refresh us and make us new on the inside. Invite those who are dry, those who are needing refreshment, those who don't know Jesus, who have not yet 'tasted' of God, to go and take a drink and see that God, does indeed satisfy.

Have a time of praise and worship and celebrate the fact that Jesus does bring refreshment and life even in the midst of deep dryness. Invite people during the worship to come and tell you what happened to them as they drank in the

water and received prayer. If you feel some of the stories
would be encouraging to others, ask people to share publicly
what happened in the meeting. If they are too shy to do that,
then perhaps suggest you interview them. If they are still too
shy, relay their story for them. This will not only encourage
people to continue to worship God but will also give you
another opportunity to ask people to go to the tables and
ask for prayer.

3 Come and Taste

THE PREPARATION

Arrange three tables to be placed at various points throughout your venue. Each table should have plates laden with luscious fruit, cut into pieces so that it is easy to eat with the hands. Once organised, cover the fruit with tin foil to keep it fresh. Make sure you organise this just before people are ready to come into the building.

Arrange for several people to look after the tables, making sure that they are not touched throughout the meeting. You will need about four people at each table because at the end of the meeting you will use them to pray for others who come to the table. Explain to these people that each table has a different subject and they should be prepared to pray about that particular subject.

Table 1 is for people who want to come to know Jesus for the first time. It is also a place to receive healing: healing of the memories, healing from hurts of the past, emotional and physical healing. Instruct those on this table that they should always ask people approaching their table if they are a Christian, because when we have used this idea in the past, there have always been people who have given their lives to Christ.

Table 2 is for people who want to pray for their family or friends to become Christians.

Table 3 is for people who want to pray for their job or their finances.

If you wish, you can choose your own subjects for the three tables in order to fit in with your own themes for the event.

If possible, arrange for the following verses to be displayed on the overhead or video screen at the appropriate time:

- Psalm 34:8
- Exodus 3:7–8
- Deuteronomy 28:1–14

Arrange for someone with a good clear voice to read the above verses at the appropriate time.

Be prepared or ask someone to talk for a short time on the subject of God calling the Israelites out of Egypt and promising to take them to the land of milk and honey.

THE IDEA

At the beginning of the meeting explain to people that your theme is the verse 'Taste and see that the Lord is good.' Ask your prearranged person to read Exodus 3:7–8. Give your prepared talk on the subject of God calling the Israelites out of Egypt and promising to take them to a land of milk and honey. Speak about the comparison of God calling us out of the kingdom of darkness and into the kingdom of light. Envision people that the promised land is a place full of God's blessing for us if we follow wholeheartedly after him. Read Deuteronomy 28:1–14, which talks of God's blessings for us if we put obedience to him at the top of our agenda. At the end of the message, challenge people to ask themselves how hungry they are for God. Tell them that we serve a loving God who is keen to bless his people. Exhort people to believe God for blessings in their lives.

Point out to people that there are tables laden with fruit throughout the room. As you are talking, the wrappers should be taken off and the fruit displayed. Explain that the fruit represents the blessings of God for our lives. If someone wants to give their life to Christ, rededicate their life to God or indeed if they want healing of a physical or emotional nature, then they should go to Table 1. If someone wants to pray for their family or friends who are not yet Christians, they should go to Table 2. If they want God to bless them in their job or indeed in the whole area of their finances, they should go to Table 3. Invite people to go to one or more tables – whatever is appropriate for them.

Make sure that those looking after the tables ask people when they arrive if they want to be prayed for, as some people might want to pray on their own for God's blessing to come upon them. However, as experience has proved with us in the past when we have used this idea, many people do want others to pray for them. This section could go on for half-an-hour or more. Encourage people to eat the fruit as a faith gesture of eating the blessings of God for their lives or for those for whom they are praying.

4 Come and Plant

This idea is based on Matthew 17:20 and is a good way of encouraging people to put their faith in God and believe him for miracles.

THE PREPARATION

You will need to buy seeds – enough to give at least one to each person. I would suggest you buy sesame, linseed or sunflower seeds, as they are small but can be eaten.

If possible arrange for Matthew 17:20 (starting at 'I tell you the truth . . .') to be displayed on the overhead or video screen either from the beginning of the event or at the appropriate time.

THE IDEA

This is a great idea to use after teaching on the importance of having faith in God. Encourage people to come to the front and take one or two seeds in their hands. Then ask them to imagine that these seeds are seeds of faith. Ask them to take them and eat them, and as they do so pray publicly that God will plant these seeds deep in their hearts and lives. Ask God to water them and make them grow.

Encourage the people to tend these seeds carefully by remembering that God is faithful and will never let us down. Ask each person to feed and water the seed each day by reading their Bible and praying. Encourage them to use their imaginations to 'see' their seed or seeds grow and develop within them.

27

5 Come and Celebrate

A number of years ago we made the decision in NGM to hold a celebration each year to remember what God had done for us and to celebrate all that he had accomplished. We had been on a walk of faith for God to provide us with a Missions and Arts complex that would be a facility where we could train and equip people to become missionaries to tell others about Jesus throughout the world. After about three years of praying and seeking God for our centre, we eventually bought a property. We refurbished the property and then built our Arts complex in the grounds. The complex includes two recording studios, one dance studio, an IT, video and graphics room, an engineers' room, two programming rooms, a fantastic performance hall and many training rooms. It was a long hard journey but a very exciting one in which God was incredibly faithful to us. We wanted everyone who joined NGM in the future to know the story of how God miraculously provided around £3 million over a period of five years. We also wanted to set aside a special day to thank God for his amazing love and faithfulness to us.

In the Bible, God told the Israelites to hold a special celebration that would remind them of how God was incredibly faithful to them. When the Israelites came out of Egypt and placed their feet on the soil of the promised land, the first thing they did was to hold a celebration to thank God for all he had done and for all he was going to do. We hold our celebration on the day we got the keys of the property. Every 22 June everyone in NGM comes to celebrate and to thank God for his amazing goodness to us all.

You can use the following idea to remind people of the goodness of God in providing a building or to thank God for something he has done for the church as a whole.

THE PREPARATION

This idea will need a group of people to organise the day. Choose a small group of people who are good at planning. Tell the church well in advance what you are going to do, so that they can put the date in their diary. Make sure you tell them that the day is for everyone, from the youngest to the eldest. Arrange to hold your celebration in a large garden, a park, or in the grounds of the church. As our day is held in June, we have it outside and arrange for 'fun' items such as bouncy castles (for adults as well as children), inflatables (for teenagers and adults) and paddling pools (for the small children). We also arrange a barbeque or a picnic lunch for everyone. We sometimes have a table tennis competition running during the afternoon. Think through what would be good for the people of your church. What activities would bring them lots of fun and laughter?

You will need to arrange food and drinks for everyone at the celebration. Make sure you have a plentiful supply.

You will also need to ask people, perhaps those in leadership in the church, to 'tell' the story of what God has done. You may wish to arrange to have communion together and/or have an open time of prayer after the stories are told.

Arrange for someone to lead worship if appropriate.

THE IDEA

Arrange for food and drinks to be ready when people arrive at the venue. Tell people why you are celebrating today and encourage them to have a great time in feasting and relaxing together using all the 'fun' items.

After a number of hours have gone by, call the church together again. Tell the story of how God provided and then ask several people to pray and thank God for his faithfulness to you as a church. You may want to prearrange who should pray, or you could open it up for anyone to pray. You may want to include celebrating communion together. We will often finish by making a joyful noise to the Lord, encouraging people to shout, dance and celebrate together what God has done. Finish with a huge clap offering or a shout of thanksgiving to God. It is so important to celebrate the goodness of God, not only because he deserves our praise, but because it focuses the church on the faithfulness of our God.

6 Come and Fast

It is so important that we know and remember why we are meeting together as a body of believers. This idea helps to bring the aims and objectives of the church to all the members' attention and brings about a sense of belonging and responsibility. It is essential in any church that the members of the congregation take on board the vision of the church.

THE PREPARATION

Create a time in the diary, perhaps once a year, when you can get together as a church to fast and pray and to commit yourselves to God, each other and the aims and objectives of the church.

How long you fast for and how you do it is entirely flexible. Sometimes we have chosen to fast for a week together using a soup fast (eating soup only), or using a partial fast (fasting for breakfast and lunch each day and eating an evening meal), or using a continuous fast by splitting the congregation into several segments, with each segment taking a portion of the week to fast. In other words the whole week is covered but each person only fasts for a small portion before handing the baton on to someone else. You may wish to fast for only a day or so – it is entirely up to what suits your situation the best and what God lays on your heart to do.

Prepare for the fast by encouraging the whole church to get involved. Make sure they understand the do's and don'ts of fasting. (I would recommend that you read the portion in my book *Spiritual Health Workout* that talks about fasting – see Resources for details.)

Explain that there are many ways of fasting and therefore if you cannot miss food for medical or other reasons you could attempt a TV fast (not watching TV for a certain amount of time), a sleep fast (giving up sleep for a certain amount of time), or a favourite fast (not eating your favourite food or drink, etc.).

You will need to arrange a day or evening when you can meet together to celebrate and pray after the fasting is completed. Arrange for the worship band or worship leader to be ready to lead the people in a time of celebration and commitment to God and each other. Prepare a party atmosphere in the hall where the celebration is to be held, using balloons, etc. You will need people or caterers to prepare the feast. Do make sure the food is very attractive to the eye.

Ask a few people to be prepared to come and share publicly what God said during the time of fasting in relation to the church as a whole. If you have been praying about people becoming Christians, ask someone to share what they believe God has said. Make sure you check out what they are going to say beforehand, so that it can all fit well together.

Prepare a list of items to pray for, which includes the aims and objectives of the church.

THE IDEA

Arrange for each person to have the list of items for prayer. Explain that at the end of the fasting period there will be a time of feasting/celebration, where the church will be asked to come and thank God for all he has done during the time of fasting. Explain that during the celebration you will be having a time where the church as a whole will be committing themselves to God and each other to fulfil the aims and objectives of the church. State in full what the aims and objectives of the church are so that people know in advance what you are asking of them.

On your feasting day/evening make sure you have a delicious meal ready for everyone. If you have been fasting for a long time, either make sure that people have broken their fast in the morning of the event, or prepare a light meal of fruit and/or salad. Right from the beginning of the event, create an atmosphere of fun and celebration, making the event something really special.

Start by thanking God for all he has done during your fast and for the food that has been prepared. After the meal, ask your musicians and worship leader to lead the congregation in a celebration, thanking God for all he has done during the days you have fasted. At an appropriate point, ask people to come and share what God said to them as they fasted. At the end, lead the people in a huge shout of praise to God. Then go into another time of celebration, during which the church's aims should be displayed on the overhead or video screen. Lead the congregation through the aims and objectives, making sure you explain that it is entirely up to each individual whether they wish to commit themselves to these before God. Afterwards, lead the congregation in a shout to God of 'God is good! His love endures for ever.'

7 Come and Enjoy

This is an idea I have used many times in my Spiritual Health
Workshops. At first people laugh when I announce that we
are going to meditate on chocolate – no one can believe I am
being serious. However, when I start to hand round the chocolate the excitement grows. People are often thinking, 'How
can God possibly speak through chocolate?' I like to remind
them that in the Bible God spoke through an ass, and if he
can speak through an ass, he can speak through anything –
including chocolate!

After people have meditated on the chocolate they are
usually amazed at what God has said to them and how
clearly he has said it.

THE PREPARATION

Buy large bars of chocolate (I prefer to use Cadbury's as it
is liked by the majority of people and is good quality chocolate), break it into squares and put it on plates.

Have some meditative music ready to play while people
are meditating. For recommended CDs/cassettes, see the
appendix at the back of the book.

THE IDEA

Announce to your group that you are all going to meditate
on chocolate. Pass the plates round and ask people to take
one piece of chocolate each. Once everyone has a square of
chocolate, say that you are going to let them meditate for

approximately five minutes before asking some volunteers to come and share what they received from God through their piece of chocolate. Encourage them to use all their senses in this meditation. Ask them to *look* at the chocolate, to *touch* it, to *smell* it and eventually to *taste* it, and to *listen* to God to see what he has to say through it. Encourage them to write down what God says to them.

Play some instrumental music during the time of meditation. Do make sure it is played quietly and sensitively. After five minutes ask the group whether they have finished. If so, ask for two or three volunteers to tell the others in the group what they received from God. You will be amazed at what people get through a simple piece of chocolate! I am every time!

This exercise not only encourages people to use their senses to hear from God, but it also gives opportunities for them to participate, therefore building their confidence.

Touch

8 Touching the Cross

The meditation I have used in this idea brings home the reality of what Jesus has accomplished for us at the cross, and each time I have used it people have become Christians.

THE PREPARATION

You will need to purchase some red material and cut it up into small pieces (about 10 cm × 10 cm). Make sure you have enough pieces to give one to each person.

Arrange for track 3 of *Journey to the Cross*, or track 8 of the same CD/cassette, to be played at the appropriate time. Ask someone to read the 'Redemption of the Cross' meditation, making sure the person you have chosen has a good clear voice and rehearses it beforehand.

Prepare some counsellors to be ready to lead people to the Lord at the appropriate time in the event and/or have some Christian literature ready to give out to those who would like it.

THE IDEA

As people are coming into your event, hand out a small piece of red cloth to each person. At the beginning, let people know that they will need this cloth at some point during the event.

At an appropriate place, ask the people to look at their piece of red cloth as you say the following: '*I want to take you through a meditation, and as I do so I want you to allow this*

*simple piece of red cloth to open your eyes and open your ears
to the sacrifice and death of the greatest man who ever lived
and walked on the earth – Jesus.'* Then play track 3 of my CD
or cassette called *Journey to the Cross*, or if you have asked
someone to read the following meditation then play track 8,
which provides the music only.

Redemption of the Cross

Imagine the colour red, Can you see it in your mind's eye?

*Focus in on the colour – red, a symbol of his death, a symbol
of the redemptive blood of Jesus. Now close your eyes and
picture in your mind the blood coming down the face, the neck,
the arms, the back of Jesus, as a crown of thorns was plunged
deep into his head. See the blood as his back was ripped to
pieces with the horrific flogging he was given. See the blood as
nails were plunged into his hands and his feet as they nailed him
to a cross. See the blood flowing from Jesus, down the cross and
spilling onto the earth.*

*Redemption rings out! Listen to the word – the Bible tells us
that all the broken and dislocated pieces of the universe –
people and things, animals and atoms – get properly fixed and
fit together in vibrant harmonies, all because of his death, his
blood that poured down from the cross.*

*Again, imagine the colour red. See it in your mind's
eye. This time open your ears to hear the symbol of his
sacrifice.*

Let the blood speak.

*Hear him crying. Father, is there any other way? Can
redemption come any other way? I know there is no other way.*

*Open your ears. Let the blood speak. Hear him crying.
Father, Dad, where are you? Can't you hear what they are
saying? 'If you really are God's son, come down from the
cross!' Father, where are you? I give you my life.*

Redemption rings out! All the broken and dislocated pieces of the universe – people and things, animals and atoms – get properly fixed and fit together in vibrant harmonies, all because of his death, his blood that poured down from the cross.

Nancy and Ray Goudie Copyright © Engage/SGO

At the end of the meditation, pray and thank Jesus for all he accomplished on the cross for us. Thank him that the story did not end with him dying, but that three days later God raised him up from the dead and he is alive today.

If you feel it is appropriate, give an appeal for people to give their lives to Jesus. You may want to use the last section of the meditation to challenge people that no matter what they are going through in life, no matter whether they feel broken or even destroyed by others or by circumstances, because of Jesus' death they can 'get properly fixed' by him. Their lives can be made whole. They can live in vibrant harmonies. In other words, they can live the way they were intended to live in the first place – living life to the full – because of all Jesus did for us at the cross of Calvary.

After the appeal, read the following song lyrics.

Red

*What would this life be like
without you in my world?
I sit and think sometimes
but it only breaks my heart.
I could not imagine the sun and moon without the stars,
I just dream of heaven, 'coz that is where you are . . .*

*And when I feel you near
Can't contain myself.
When I hear your voice
I'm yours, always and ever.*

Red is the colour
that is deep within my heart.
Red is the love I feel,
even when we're apart.
'coz Red is never fading, bright and captivating!
Red is my delight, beautiful in every way . . .

Mark Underdown Copyright © NGM 2002

Finish the meeting with a time of worship, thanking Jesus
for all he has done for us.

9   Touching His Heart

This is an idea that has brought tremendous encouragement to all who have participated in it, but even more
importantly I believe it has brought incredible joy to the
heart of God.

It was a number of years ago, when Ray and I were leading
our first team called Heartbeat, that I discovered the joy of
writing a psalm. When someone said, 'Let's write a psalm of
praise to God,' I was horrified! I was surrounded by people
who wrote songs and that fact did nothing for my confidence. However, when I put pen to paper and I concentrated
on my heavenly Father and how much he had done for me, a
huge explosion of praise welled up in me, and I simply wrote
down what I was feeling.

My psalm was not the best poem or song that had ever
been written, but it came from my heart of praise to God
and therefore reflected who I was and my relationship with
God. As I have used this exercise in my workshops many
times, God's presence has fallen in deep ways. Writing a
psalm is not only a way of touching God's heart, but is
also a way through which God can touch us. Do try it with
your congregation or group and I am sure you will find
through this exercise that God meets with people in new
ways.

THE PREPARATION

Make sure you have spare pens and paper in case people
need them.

If possible, arrange for any psalms you read to be displayed at the appropriate time on your overhead or video screen.

THE IDEA

Let the people know that as part of your worship to God, you would like each of them to write a psalm. Encourage them that their psalm doesn't need to be the best in the world; it just needs to reflect their love and heart for God. To encourage people into this exercise, perhaps read one or both of the following psalms, which have been written by people attending my workshops. Explain that each psalm reflects the personality of the person who wrote it. Then read a psalm of praise from the Bible. Psalm 100 is a great example.

This first psalm was written by a teenage girl who attended one of my workshops and became my son Aidan's nanny – and by the way, she's mad about chocolate!

> *My God is my night and day,*
> *My moon and stars on a summer night.*
> *My God is my life and without him I'll surely die.*
>
> *My God is nicer than chocolate,*
> *Nicer than summer rain.*
> *My God is nicer than a ray of sunshine*
> *On a rainy day.*

Michelle McKenzie. Used with permission

This next psalm was written at one of my workshops in Swindon by a teenage boy and brings out clearly his sense of humour as well as his love for God. I've called it the Ready Brek psalm.

Ready Brek

Like the greatest bowl of Ready Brek,
You bring your warmth.
Like the hottest ever chilli,
You bring your fire.

Like the spring day,
You bring your beautiful creation.
Like the summer time,
You bring your joy.

In the pits of sorrow,
You bring your comfort.
In the scream of pain,
You bring your healing.
In the valley of death,
You bring your blessing.

Into the world, Lord,
You brought your Son.
To me, Lord,
You've given me hope.
To me, Lord,
You've given life.

Author unknown

While people are writing, you can play some quiet meditative music in the background if you feel this would aid
people's concentration, but make sure it does not have words
and that it is played quietly.

Allow around five minutes for people to write their
psalms, and make sure you inform people beforehand how
much time they have. At the end of the allotted time, ask if

everyone has finished. If so, ask for a couple of volunteers to come up and read their psalm to the group. This exercise will not only encourage everyone to worship God individually, but will also bring a huge sense of worship into the meeting. You can sense God smile on the meeting as he hears how his children love and worship him.

10 Touching Prayer

Personally, I have found walking as I pray to be extremely helpful. However, this idea goes much further. We in NGM have often used this method of prayer with brilliant results.

THE PREPARATION

If you are going to be walking around your own building, you won't have much to prepare. However, if you are going to walk around your local town, clubs, pubs, park, etc., you will need to think through how you will do that. You will also need oil to anoint the land.

THE IDEA

If you are praying for God to impact a local area, then one way of doing that is to pray as you walk around the boundaries. You may or may not wish to bring it to the attention of the local residents. If you wish to let them know that you are praying for them, then do inform the local police as to what you are doing as a church and perhaps arrange for the local papers to take photos of the church as they walk. Make sure you have an appointed spokesperson who can answer the questions from the press as to why you are doing a prayer walk.

Often local people will be thrilled that the church cares enough to pray for the good of the town. However, in some circumstances it may not be wise to let the local area know that you are prayer walking. In those circumstances, arrange for your people to be split into groups of three or four and release them at five-minute intervals from the church to go to the particular place where you want to pray. When they reach the place they should pray around the building or area, reaching out to God for anything he wants to impart to you as a church at that time. When they arrive back at the church, or where they started from, people should report what they felt as they prayed and what God said to them.

If you are about to build a new church building or venue, it would be good to ask the members of the church to walk round the site and pray for a release of God's Spirit onto the land. Anoint the land with oil. Pray and lay hands on it, asking God to make the land 'fruitful' and for many people to become Christians through the work in your new building. Again, ask people to share what they received from God as they prayed around the site and anointed the foundations with oil.

11   Touching Faith

This idea comes from John 12:24 where Jesus says, 'I tell you the truth, unless a grain of wheat falls to the ground and dies, it remains only a single seed. But if it dies, it produces many seeds.' You can use this idea to encourage people in their faith to pray and to 'see' friends and family become Christians.

THE PREPARATION

You will need to provide one plastic cup and one or two seeds for each person coming to your event. You will also need enough clean potting compost to half-fill each cup. Have several places in the venue where you have the compost and the plastic cups set out ready to use at the appropriate time. Keep the seeds with you at the front of the meeting.

THE IDEA

You can use this idea as part of a faith-building talk or as a response at the end. After encouraging people to believe God will break into situations in their own family, friends and neighbours' lives, ask them to go to the tables and take one cup and half-fill it with soil. Then ask them to take one or two seeds and, as an act of faith, plant the seed in the soil, believing that as the seed falls into the ground and dies, it will bear much fruit. Ask them to pray for their friends, family, neighbours, town, city or nation as they plant their seeds.

After everyone has done this, ask one of your leaders to

pray for God's Spirit to come, and for each person to see the fruit of their prayers in time. Encourage them to look for signs of life in their friends and family and tell them not to get discouraged when they don't see things happen quickly. Roots have to grow underneath the surface before we begin to see the new life appear.

12 Touching Jesus

This idea works well after preaching a message about our desperation for God.

THE PREPARATION

You will need some small pieces of cloth about 10 cm × 10 cm in size – one for each person. Try and find some cloth of a similar material to the robe that Jesus would possibly have worn 2000 years ago. When I used this idea at my Spiritual Health conferences we bought Indian cotton, which was ideal. Give the material out as people arrive.

Prepare a message about our hunger for God. Perhaps base it on the story in Luke 8:42–48.

THE IDEA

Tell people that the piece of cloth they were given when they arrived will be used later during the message.

At the appropriate time in your event, preach your message about the woman who was desperate to touch Jesus. Ask people how desperate they are today for God. Are they desperate to get close to him, to touch him, to meet with him, to receive his power? Explain how this woman was so desperate to meet with Jesus that even though there were many people surrounding him (probably thousands) she was determined to fight her way through. She probably got knocked around – she may even have been tripped up, trampled on and crushed – but she did not give up. She continued to push through, because she was desperate.

Again, challenge your audience. Are they desperate for God, for intimacy with him? Do they really want to know him? If we are desperate we act differently. Give an illustration about pictures people may have seen on their television screens at certain times of starving people during a famine. Explain that when food comes into their town or village, the starving people don't just stand around saying, 'Oh, that's nice! I'm glad the food is here!' They push and shove and even fight for the food, because they are desperate. Challenge your audience, 'Are you starving for God? If so, you will be eager for more of God and it will show in what you do.'

At the end of your talk, ask people to hold the piece of cloth given to them earlier. Explain that when you pray, you want them to tell God how desperate they are for him. Ask them to use the cloth as a tool to help them to cling on to Jesus, just as the woman did many years ago. Remind them that she received healing through touching the hem of his garment. Ask them to use their imaginations as they pray to see themselves touch the hem of Jesus' garment and at that point tell Jesus what they need from him. The woman needed healing, but there may be some among you who need forgiveness, while others may need a fresh touch of the Holy Spirit. Whatever people need from God, encourage them as they touch his garment to ask God to release it to them.

Spend the next few moments praying corporately and individually before concluding the meeting with a time of praise and worship.

13 Touching the Spirit

THE PREPARATION

You will need oil to anoint people. I suggest using fragrant oil, which you can purchase from the Body Shop or somewhere similar. Choose one that is suitable for both men and women.

You will need to prepare several leaders to pray for others, with at least one leader to pray for each topic. Try and pick leaders who are in the same line of work, for example a leader who is a businessman to pray for those who are working in the business field.

THE IDEA

At an appropriate point in your event, ask those who are involved in business (or who are planning to be) to line up facing the leader who is going to pray for them. Do the same with those in full-time education (whether teachers or students), those in the arts and media, full-time Christian work and any other areas you may wish to add, depending on what kind of group you have. You may wish to pick a few main areas and then have one for people who are not involved in any of those mentioned.

Ask them to come one by one to be prayed for by the appropriate person at the front. That leader should anoint them with oil and pray for them, asking that God would use them to be salt and light within the area they work. Depending on how many are waiting to be prayed for, you could have two or more lines, provided you have the leaders ready to pray and anoint with oil.

Once three or so have been prayed for, encourage them to get into groups and pray for each other until everyone at the event has been prayed for.

14 Touching the World

This idea was brought to me by a friend called Jonny Sertin and used in a conference called Remix a number of years ago. It is ideal to use after you have been encouraging people to get involved in evangelism or helping with the homeless, the disadvantaged, etc.

THE PREPARATION

You will need a bag of clean compost – enough for everyone to take a handful. Put the bag at the front of the venue with old newspapers or a plastic cover underneath so it is easy to clear up later.

THE IDEA

At the beginning, before your talk, ask people to come forward and take a handful of soil. Ask them to rub their hands in the dirt and then go back to their seats. Then talk about the importance of getting our hands dirty for God.

During your talk, ask how many people would like to be able to wash their hands and feel clean again. I'm sure a lot would say that this was the case. Explain that when we get involved in Kingdom business, we will often get our hands dirty, and therefore at times we will want to wash our hands of what is going on. However, in order to see the kingdom established it is important that we keep going and do not give up – even if it is uncomfortable for us. Emphasise that it would be far easier for us just to give up and wash our hands, but God wants to encourage us to keep on going and see the work through.

15   Touching Others Through the Word

I believe it is so important to encourage people to read the Bible. This creative idea not only encourages people to explore their Bible, but also encourages them to pray.

THE PREPARATION

You will need a prayer from Scripture that you can use as an example. There are many prayers in the Bible and these are just a few:

- John 17
- Ephesians 1:17–19
- Ephesians 3:16–19
- Philippians 1:9–11

The Psalms are also full of prayers.

THE IDEA

Ask people to get into pairs. Explain that you would like each person to pray for their partner using their Bible to find a prayer that they would like to pray. Explain that the Bible is full of prayers and give them some ideas, showing them an example by praying the prayer as you want them to pray it for their partner. For example, if their partner's name was Lucy this is how they might pray using Ephesians 3:16–19: 'I pray that out of his glorious riches he may strengthen you, Lucy, with power through his Spirit in your inner being, so

that Christ may dwell in your heart by faith. And I pray that
you, Lucy, being rooted and established in love, may have
power, together with all the saints, to grasp how wide and
long and high and deep is the love of Christ, and I pray that
you, Lucy, will know this love that surpasses knowledge –
that you, Lucy, may be filled to the measure of all the fullness of God.'

Explain to people that they will have about ten to fifteen
minutes to find a prayer from the Bible and to pray it for
their partner.

Smell

16 The Aroma of Life

How many of you have walked past a bakery, smelled the aroma of freshly baked bread and been tempted to walk inside to eat or buy some bread? Arousing the senses in the area of smell can be advantageous to us all as we come into the presence of God. In the Old Testament, we are told that when the priests went into the holy place to worship the Lord, smell played an important part. There was the smell of the incense, which they burned before the Lord, and the smell of the sacrifice.

Smell can also bring back memories. When you smell a certain smell it can remind you of something that happened to you many years ago.

THE PREPARATION

Find one or two good quality bottles of eau de toilette with men and women in mind. Do make sure that the perfume you choose is delightful to smell. Ask a number of people for their opinion.

Ask a couple of your leaders, or people who have a passion to pray for others, if they would pray for people at the end of the event.

Buy some white cardboard and cut it into small strips.

THE IDEA

This is a creative idea that came through Zoë Wickham, who works with me at NGM. I have used it at my Spiritual Health

Weekends to create a lasting memory in people's minds of what God did for them during any particular meeting.

After the talk, or at an appropriate place in your programme, invite people to come forward for prayer. Arrange for your leaders or counsellors to be stationed at various points in the venue. When people come forward, the counsellors should ask them if they have any specific thing they would like prayer for. Before praying for them, the counsellors should ask them if they would mind if they sprayed them with perfume. (They could be given the choice of having it on their wrists or on a small piece of card.) After spraying the perfume, the counsellor should then ask them to smell it before proceeding to pray for them. They should pray for the smell of the presence of the Lord to come upon them, asking God to permeate his smell deep into their hearts and lives; that the very smell of heaven would come upon them and that every time they smell that smell it would remind them not only that God is with them but also what God did for them through the event and through the prayers.

17 The Aroma of Bread

THE PREPARATION

Buy a number of freshly baked loaves of bread, choosing a selection that easily stimulates the sense of smell. Try and arrange to collect the bread just before the event starts.

Place the loaves on clean plates on tables covered by a tablecloth or tin foil. Make sure your arrangement is pleasant to the eye and appropriate to the age of your group. Have your tables placed at various points throughout the room.

THE IDEA

The smell of freshly baked bread can often stimulate the sense of hunger in a person. In this idea, we use the smell of bread to remind people of their need to be hungry for God. Bread also speaks of life, and in this idea we want to remind people that the only way to fulfil their potential in life is to reach out and touch the Lord Jesus.

At the beginning of the meeting, explain to people that the bread is there to stimulate their hunger for God. Invite them to come and eat some bread at any point during the meeting. If during the worship or any other part of the event they want to say to God, 'God, I am hungry for you,' or 'God, I want more of you,' then they should go to a table and take a piece of bread as a declaration that they are hungry for God. At the end of the event invite people again to come and eat the bread. If you feel it is appropriate, then prearrange for

counsellors to be available at the tables at the end to pray
with those who wish prayer.

This idea not only reminds people of their desire to reach
out for God and to increase in hunger for God, but also
encourages people to do something about what they feel
deep within themselves. So many people cannot verbalise
their hunger for God, but putting their feelings into action
will often help them to cement their relationship with their
heavenly Father.

18 The Aroma of Purity

THE PREPARATION

Prepare several bowls of clean warm water to be placed at several points throughout your venue. Beside each bowl, place some fragrant soap and a couple of small towels. (Remember to choose soap that is appropriate for both men and women.)

THE IDEA

At the end of your meeting invite people to come forward and wash their hands in the bowls provided, as a sign that they want to be cleansed by the washing of the Spirit of God. As they wash their hands, ask them to pray inwardly for God to cleanse them and renew them within. If appropriate, ask for some counsellors to be stationed at each bowl in case people want to be prayed for at the end of their cleansing that the Holy Spirit would come and fill them. You will sometimes get people coming to be cleansed by God for the first time, so prepare counsellors to pray people through into the kingdom of God. However, do not restrict the exercise to people who want to give their lives to God or people who wish to rededicate their lives to Jesus. Many of us, no matter how long we have been Christians or how deeply we love the Lord, need God to come and cleanse us. It may simply be a wrong thought, word or deed – so encourage all to come and wash their hands as a symbol of a deeper cleansing within.

When people have finished, encourage them to smell their hands. They should smell fresh and new – a symbol of their newness and freshness in Christ.

We have discovered as we have used this idea that significant things can happen to many individuals as they recognise their need for God to come and cleanse them, renew them and fill them again with his Holy Spirit.

19 The Aroma of Humility

When this idea has been used in the past, it has been amazing to see how God breaks through and impacts people. Relationships have been restored and many hurts healed through the simple act of serving each other by washing each other's feet.

THE PREPARATION

You will need to prepare several bowls of lukewarm water, with enough cloths and towels for each person and fragrant oil or cream beside each one. Do remember that you will be using the oil/cream on both men and women, so it might be appropriate to purchase two fragrances.

It would be advisable for people to come prepared, wearing suitable clothing.

If possible, arrange for John 13:1–17 to be displayed on the video or overhead screen at the appropriate time.

Spend time praying beforehand that God will speak through this idea and that barriers will be broken down between the generations and the genders, etc.

THE IDEA

At the appropriate place in your event read John 13:1–17, which is the story of Jesus washing the feet of his disciples. If possible, arrange for the text to be displayed on the video or overhead screen so that people can follow it, even if they don't have their Bibles.

There are several ways to do this idea. You could ask each of your leaders to take a bowl, towels, etc., and then wash the feet of people in the congregation, thus copying what the Lord did to his disciples. (Use a fresh soaked cloth for each person so there is no need for them to put their feet into the water.) Another way of doing it is to ask the fathers and mothers in the group to wash the feet of their children, or instead of parents you could ask several older people to wash the teenagers' feet. I have only seen this happen once, but when it did there was a huge breakthrough in relationships between the old and the young, as well as parents and children. It could be a very significant time in terms of relationships between those who are so misunderstood. However, it is important that no pressure is exerted on those who do not wish to take part.

Another significant way of using this idea is to ask the men to wash the feet of the women. In our society, and many times within the church, women can feel trodden on rather than valued. This is a way of showing the women that they are not just there to serve but that the men value the women and are willing to serve them. This idea would obviously work best in small groups where the men and women know each other reasonably well and are comfortable with one another, rather than embarrassed.

Ask those who are washing others' feet to gently wash them with a soaked cloth and then apply the fragrant oil or cream. Use an oil or cream that has a pleasant smell and you will find that as it is used a pleasing aroma will arise within the venue. Not only will it feel pleasant to the touch, but each time the person smells that fragrance thereafter he or she will remember the act of kindness shown.

20 The Aroma of Prayer

Prayer is the key to revival. If we want to see God move in
revival power and be part of it, we need to be encouraging
people to pray. One way to do that is to make our prayer
meetings interesting, creative and exciting. After all, talking
to God, the one who made the universe, is one of the most
exciting things we can do. Yet often the church prayer
meeting is the least attended service in the church calendar.
This idea will give a real focus for prayer and allow everyone
in the event to be included.

THE PREPARATION

You will need to allocate four areas of your room for the
prayer points. One area will be allocated as the worship
point, another as the repentance point, a third as a place
where we can pray for family and friends and a fourth for
praying for the nation and for God to move and bring
revival.

Make each point special by decorating that part of the
venue in keeping with its title. I will give you suggested items
that will help you get started, but you may wish to add to
them or decorate in a way that complements your prayer
event.

If you are using this idea for a small group meeting in your
home and you don't have sufficient room in your lounge, you
may want to consider, if you can, using four rooms of your
home.

Worship point

Print various verses of Scripture on paper and stick them to the wall or put them on a large board. For example, 1 Chronicles 16 is a great psalm of praise. If you cannot put up the whole psalm, use the following verses: 1 Chronicles 16:8–13, 23–34, 36. Have a board or a flip chart where people can write their comments or Scripture references.

Have worship music playing in the background – not necessarily music with words, but music that encourages people to be drawn into the presence of God. Please see Resources for suggested music.

Perhaps light a candle and put some cushions on the floor to make it easier for people to kneel in worship if they wish to do so.

Buy some incense (use the smell of frankincense or myrrh if you are able).

Repentance point

Build an altar of stones and place various candles around it. Put a cross or a picture of a cross in a central point beside the altar. Again, you can display some verses that talk about the forgiving nature of our God, e.g. 1 John 1:9.

If you wish you could display the following self-check list, which is taken from my book, *Spiritual Health Workout* (see Resources for details).

Self-check list

Go through the following list. All of these pervade our nation. Spend some time asking God to reveal if any of these are in your heart and life. Be prepared to allow God, who truly sees our hearts, to highlight any areas you cannot see.

1. Selfishness
2. Pride

3. Negativity
4. Critical spirit
5. Lacking in love/hardness of heart
6. Bitterness
7. Envy/jealousy
8. Lying (even saying half truths)
9. Impatience
10. Lacking in kindness
11. Slander (speaking about people behind their backs)
12. Anger
13. Fear
14. Lacking in joy
15. Confusion
16. Rejection (of others, God, self, etc.)
17. Rebellion
18. Lacking in generosity

Have some paper and pens available so that people can write down things they wish to bring before God in repentance. Also have a big waste paper basket where people can throw their paper as a declaration that their sin is gone and they are forgiven.

Display some bread on a table. Make sure the bread is fresh as we want the smell of the bread to speak to people about their own hunger for God.

Friends and family point

At this point place verses that talk of the love of God on the wall or on a chart. Display verses that talk of God's faithfulness to us and his promise which is for us, our children and our children's children (e.g. Deuteronomy 28:3–6; Isaiah 44:3; Jeremiah 31:3; John 3:16; Acts 2:38–39).

Have a piece of paper either on the wall or on a flip chart where people can write the names of those they are praying for.

For this section, and also the section for revival, make sure you have plenty of space for people to walk about and pray.

Revival point

Cover the walls with pictures that depict the world we live in. Include some showing the youth culture, businessmen in suits, old people, those in government, etc. Try looking in newspapers and magazines for these. Display words such as 'the media', 'television', 'newspapers', 'the record industry', 'show business', 'education', 'poverty', 'drugs', 'violence' and 'homelessness'.

Light a few fragrant candles and have the smell permeate the area where you are praying for revival as a reminder that the smell of God transcends all barriers and that God's Spirit can move across various cultures and age groups.

THE IDEA

At the beginning of the event, explain that you are going to spend the next hour or so praying and seeking God in a new and creative way. Bring people's attention to the four different prayer points and explain the function of each.

Worship – a place to worship and praise God; to give to God what he deserves; to thank him for all he has done and all that he is going to do; to honour him for all he has done in each of our lives.

Bring people's attention to the flip chart or board and explain that they may wish to write their praise and worship down, or perhaps write an encouraging psalm of praise (see Idea 9). Inform them that the candle is lit to remind them that God is present with us and his Holy Spirit is within.

If you are using incense that smells of frankincense or myrrh, tell people that the fragrance in the worship point is the same fragrance that was brought to Jesus at his birth.

The wise men came to worship the young King, bringing with them gold, frankincense and myrrh (Matthew 2:1–11).

Repentance – a place to come in repentance to God for any wrong thought or deed that he highlights. Ask people to start by praying individually and asking God to transport them to the Holy of Holies. Encourage them to use their imagination to come into the presence of God. While in God's presence encourage them to ask God to bring to their mind anything they have done or said that did not please him. If you have displayed the above check list, then ask each person to go through the list one by one and ask God to highlight any of these things in their lives. They should write down anything that God highlights on a piece of paper. After confession and receiving God's forgiveness, get them to rip up the paper and place it in the bin as a visible sign that God has forgiven them.

At the end of their time, invite people to eat a small portion of the bread as a declaration to him of their hunger for him to move in their lives. Remind them to smell the bread before eating and allow the smell to awaken 'hunger' within them. Ask them to pray for a deeper hunger for God in their lives.

Friends and family – a place to bring our friends and family to God and ask him to move powerfully in their lives. Inform people that this is the point where you would like them to pray for their friends and family who as yet do not know Jesus. Ask them to bring them to God in prayer and perhaps write their name on the paper or flip chart that you have provided.

Revival – a place to pray for revival in ourselves, our church, our nation and the nations of the world. Encourage people to cry out for God to bring revival, praying especially for the

areas they see on the walls or on the flip chart, e.g. the
government, the Royal family or president, the media, the
youth, the business world. Ask them to write down anything
they receive from God and to be prepared to tell everyone
what they got at the end, Ask them to use their imaginations
as they pray, to see the very smell of God beginning to permeate through the different cultures and age groups they are
praying for.

About fifteen to twenty minutes before the meeting should
end, call everyone together again and ask people to give
reports on what God said to them at any of the four points.
This should be an encouraging time, a time of building
everyone up and increasing their faith. Finish the evening in
prayer and encourage people to let you know of any answers
to prayer in the coming days or weeks.

21   The Aroma of His Spirit

This is a simple idea that you can use not only in church events but also in small groups such as committee meetings, cells or meetings held in the home.

THE PREPARATION

You will need a reasonably large candle, preferably one that has a nice smell to it. Buy or borrow a tall candle holder, or place the candle on a table so that it will be seen by everyone.

THE IDEA

Light a candle at the beginning of your meeting, explaining to all present that it is there to remind them that the Holy Spirit is present. Whether it is during the talk or during discussion (in a committee meeting), it is good to remind ourselves that the God of the impossible is present with us. Explain that each time they look at the candle, they should be reminded that God is present with them and wants to pervade their lives.

This is a simple idea, and yet very effective. When my husband, Ray, first suggested this idea for our NGM meetings and leadership meetings, I found it to be very inspiring, helpful and faith-building throughout all our discussions.

22 The Aroma of His Presence

This idea works well if you want to concentrate on the subject of intimacy with God. The aim is to bring people into the throne room of God – to have them come into a deeper experience of God. You can use this idea on its own, or as part of a talk to encourage people to deeper intimacy.

THE PREPARATION

You will need to buy some incense, perhaps frankincense or myrrh. Make sure you have enough of it so that the fragrance fills the venue.

You will also need some background music, preferably with no words, to play during the readings below. I would recommend track 6 of my CD *A God Encounter*.

Ask your worship leader or band, or be prepared yourself, to lead worship and praise where appropriate.

THE IDEA

Read 1 Kings 8:10–11. Bring to everyone's attention the fact that the priests could not continue with their service. They had to stop because the presence of God was so strong. The cloud of his presence had so filled the temple that it was impossible for their service to continue. Encourage people to cry out to God; to speak out their prayers for him to come and be present at the service. Ask them to pray together out loud that God's presence would fill the room and his smell would so impact their lives that not only would it be life-changing, but God would impact others through them.

Read Hebrews 10:19–22. Encourage people to come into the throne room of God.

Read Revelation 4 and then ask everyone to close their eyes as you read the following:

The Throne Room

Use your imagination – use the eyes of your heart to see a door in front of you standing open. As you look, a voice seems to say to you, 'Come.' Your heart responds 'Yes' and at once you are in the throne room of the almighty God. You are stunned and amazed by the colours – purples, greens and reds as you have never seen them before. Surrounding the throne is what looks like a rainbow and the one who sits on the throne has the appearance of jasper, amber and gold. Just in front of the throne is what looks like a sea of glass, pure and clear like crystal.

Take a few minutes to listen to God. Hear what he has to say to you. Listen to his voice. Allow his words to penetrate your mind and stimulate your heart. (Leave a few moments of the music only, then read the following.)

All around the throne are thousands and thousands of people shouting and singing their praises to the holy living God. They shout, 'You are worthy, O God, to receive glory and honour and power, for you created all things and by your will they were created and have their being. Holy, Holy, Holy is the Lord God Almighty.'

At this point, encourage people to shout their praises to God. Encourage them to tell God that he is amazing, that he is worthy, that he deserves all the praise. Ask the band or worship leader to lead the people in a song of praise to God, perhaps ending with a huge clap offering to God (applause).

Then encourage people to come to the front and share what they felt God was saying, or pray aloud what is on their heart. They may ask for prayer for healing or any other area where they want God to move, whether in their life or in the lives of others.

Just before the end of the event, read Exodus 34:29 where it talks of Moses coming from the presence of God and people noticing that his face was shining with the glory of God. Encourage people again to pray out loud together that as they leave the event or meeting God's smell would go with them; that the fragrance and light of Jesus would be on them and that people would notice a difference in their lives.

Hearing

23   The Bible Speaks

One of the lost arts in the Christian world is meditation, yet so many people these days are trying to find peace, joy and fulfilment through that very art form. However, many of them are looking for answers to life's problems through exploring the wrong kind of meditation. As Christians, we know that the original form of meditation is the only kind that will ultimately bring us in touch with ourselves and the living God. Christian meditation is a wonderful refreshing way of hearing God speak to us and has been used for thousands of years.

The Bible contains many references to meditation – you can find it mentioned from the beginning to the end of the book. Yet because Transcendental Meditation, the New Age movement and Eastern mysticism have so hi-jacked our creative gift, we tend to shy away from using it at all.

I am going to give you several ways of hearing from God through Christian meditation and I am praying that as you use these in your churches, events or small groups, God will not only help you to hear him more clearly, but will also bring you into a deeper and more intimate walk with him.

THE PREPARATION

If you can, arrange for the instructions on how to meditate and the meditation verse below to be displayed on the overhead or video screen. If you are using this idea in a small group held in a home, either print the instructions out on paper, or buy copies of this book or my *Spiritual Health*

Workout book, so that each person has a copy of the instructions on how to meditate. Instead of putting the verse on the screen, you can ask people to use their Bibles.

You will also need to make sure that each person has a pen and paper. Bring some extra pens and a pad of paper, just in case you need them. It may be good to have extra Bibles as well.

Choose some quiet meditative music without words to play in the background. (See Resources for recommended recordings.)

THE IDEA

At the beginning of this exercise, encourage people that each one of them, no matter where they are in their walk with God, will be able to hear God clearly through meditation. If they have never meditated before, display the following instructions on the overhead or video screen and go through the instructions with them, explaining each one. You will find that the instructions are very simple and therefore do not need a lot of explanation, but do make sure everyone is clear before you start.

How to Meditate

1. Look up the suggested scripture in your Bible.
2. Read it.
3. Pray and ask God to speak to you through this verse.
4. Read it again several times.
5. Spend time thinking about what the verse says.
6. Perhaps dwell on a phrase or section of the verse, or even just one word.
7. Allow yourself to follow a train of thought until you see something in the verse you have never seen before, or God highlights something in a new or fresh way.

8. Write down what you receive.
9. If your mind begins to wander totally off the subject, start again at number one.

Do make sure people understand that as they are meditating God may highlight a phrase or word in the verse, just as he sometimes does when we are reading our Bibles. As their attention is drawn to that particular phrase or word then they should allow themselves to follow a train of thought until they discover what God is trying to say. Encourage them to trust the thoughts that come into their heads and to write down what they feel God is saying.

Display the following verse on the overhead or video screen (or if you are in a home then ask your group to look up the verse in their Bibles) and let people know that you are giving them about five minutes to meditate on this verse and you will then pick some volunteers to share with everyone what they received from God. As they begin to meditate, perhaps play some quiet meditative music (without words) in the background.

Meditation Verse

I am the vine; you are the branches. If a man remains in me and I in him, he will bear much fruit; apart from me you can do nothing.
(John 15:5)

A minute or so before the five minutes finish, remind people to begin to write down what they are receiving from God and say you will be bringing this time to a close in a couple of minutes.

When you feel the time is right, ask for a couple of volunteers to come up to the front and share what they got from this verse. After hearing what God has said to the first two

84 HEARING

volunteers, ask if anyone else received something similar. Then ask if anyone received something completely different. If people respond, ask a couple of volunteers to share their thoughts from God. If you have a large audience, you could then get them into small groups to share all their meditations and begin to pray for one another out of what they received. Alternatively, you could choose another verse to meditate on, thus encouraging them to build on what they have learned. This exercise could be used on its own or as part of a bigger programme.

24 Fruit Speaks

This is an idea I have used many times in my Spiritual Health Conferences as a method of hearing God speak to us through his creation. The Bible is full of references to fruit, and it is interesting to note that fruit is mentioned in the first and last chapters of the Bible. Throughout Scripture God has spoken to us again and again through fruit.

THE PREPARATION

Before the programme begins, prepare several trays of fruit. Choose apples, strawberries, oranges, kiwi fruit, pears, grapes and perhaps little boxes of raisins. Make sure you have enough fruit on the trays so that people can have one item each.

Play some quiet reflective music in the background as people meditate on the fruit. I would suggest either of my meditation recordings, *Journey to the Cross* or *A God Encounter*, or any music that does not have words.

THE IDEA

Explain at the start that you would like everyone to meditate and hear God speak through fruit. Nominate some people to pass round the fruit, and ask each person to pick one fruit from the tray.

Then explain to them that they should use all their faculties and not just taste. Encourage them to look at the fruit, to touch and feel it, to smell it before tasting it, while asking

God to speak to them through it. Let them know how long you are allowing in the programme for them to reach out and hear from God. I would suggest that this needs to be at least five minutes, but it would be good to check if everyone has finished before asking for volunteers to come forward to share what they received from God through their fruit. Explain that you will have some reflective meditative music playing in the background to help them focus.

Before you begin, ask God to speak clearly to everyone individually through these pieces of fruit.

After five minutes or so, ask for volunteers to come forward to share what they received from God through the fruit. I'm sure you will be amazed at what God says through this type of meditation.

25 Nature Speaks

THE PREPARATION

Before the event begins, prepare several trays containing different expressions of nature, such as flowers, twigs, stones, glasses of water, acorns, leaves. Make sure there is an object for each person.

If possible, arrange for the verse to be displayed on the overhead or video screen at the right time. If you feel it is appropriate then play some meditative music. I would suggest my recordings *Journey to the Cross* and/or *A God Encounter*, as they provide music without words.

THE IDEA

Introduce this idea by saying that you are going to meditate on some aspects of nature. Display Psalm 24:1 on the overhead or video screen. You don't need to refer to it, unless you feel you would like to. It is more of a declaration. If you are unable to use an overhead or video, you may want to read the verse aloud to your group.

If your group has not meditated before, make sure you explain how to do it (see Idea 23 for instructions). Encourage each person to reach out to God and to hear something from him for themselves. Remind them to write down what they hear from him through the meditation. I know they will be amazed at how much God can reveal of himself through nature. If appropriate, play the quiet meditative music at this point.

Inform people that you will be asking for volunteers afterwards to share what they received from God through their meditation. Also announce how long they have to meditate (I would suggest around five to ten minutes). Just before the time is up, remind people that they should be writing down their meditative thoughts, and say that you will be bringing the whole session to a close in a couple of minutes.

At the end of the meditation, ask for volunteers to come and share what they received. If you feel it is necessary, ask a few people beforehand to be prepared to come and share, in case no one has the courage to come to the front. Once a couple of people come and share you will find that others are keen to come and share what they received from God too. Ask them to bring their leaf, twig, flower or other object with them to show the audience what they meditated on.

26 Creativity Speaks

Trish Morgan, who was a lead singer in our band Heartbeat back in the 1980s, was the first person to suggest that we use this idea. When she laid down hammers, screwdrivers, etc. on the floor in front of us and asked us to reach out to God for each other, we thought she had gone mad! But through her creativity, God spoke clearly to us.

Many people find it difficult to hear from God, yet at my Spiritual Health Weekends, when I encourage people to reach out and hear God for themselves through the various exercises, they are amazed at how easily the voice of God seems to come to them.

I have used this exercise many times to help people tune in to the voice of God, not for themselves but for the others within their group. When I have used it, many have not only heard God for the first time, but have also had the courage to share with others what they received. This idea will encourage people at all stages of their walk with God to reach out and listen to God's voice.

THE PREPARATION

Before the event, prepare trays of objects. These objects can include anything you happen to have around your home: paper, pen, pencil, sticky tape, eraser, screwdriver, torch, highlighter pen, lamp, glass, hammer, etc. Make sure you have enough objects for everyone in each group.

THE IDEA

Ask people to get into groups of six to eight. If you are using this idea for a small group, divide the people up only if you feel it is appropriate. When all groups are ready, place an object tray on the floor in the middle of each group. Inform them that you want them to reach out to God using one of these objects, listening to him for an encouraging word for someone in their group. Explain that you are not looking for directive words for anyone, but something encouraging or something that will build them up.

Once they have heard from God for someone else, encourage them to pick up the object and give it to the person before telling them what they received and praying for them. After they have finished, ask them to put the object back on the tray. Explain that the same object can be used more than once. Pray from the front for people's ears to be open to the living God. Explain how much time they have available to hear from God and give their word of encouragement. When I have used this idea in the past it can take twenty minutes or more to complete.

While they are reaching out to God and receiving words for each other, ask two or three of your leaders to go round the groups listening to see how they are getting on. If people have not started to give out their words, they should be encouraged to do so. If they are finding it difficult, the leader should stay with that group, answer their questions, reach out to God and show them by example how it is done.

27 Music Speaks

THE IDEA

One of the ideas we have used in NGM during the last few years is playing music while someone is speaking or preaching. We have used this idea in evangelistic settings particularly with young people, but also in teaching sessions in the church with great results.

With the club culture of today, this idea resonates with the unchurched youth particularly well. We have used CDs and cassettes, mostly of our own music (see Resources for CDs/cassettes you could purchase which would work well in this setting). However, we often use our NGM DJs to do a live mix. We have around fifteen DJs working within NGM and many of them have been trained to be very sensitive in this kind of situation. I have often worked with Andy Hunter (NGM DJ) both in evangelism and also in teaching situations. When Andy and I have worked together, many people have come up to me at the end and asked how long we took to rehearse. When we say the only rehearsal we have is our prayer time together, they are amazed! God seems to blend our skills so well. However, having said that, just as I would spend time alone with God preparing to preach, Andy would prepare by asking God for the right combination of music to communicate God's heart in any given situation.

Instead of distracting people, I find the music adds to the message and people are touched in all areas of their senses. I have used 'Braveheart' music as well as our own NGM

CDs/cassettes. It is important to make sure, however, that the music is not too loud for you or your audience. It should be in the background, yet not so quiet that people cannot hear it.

28 Revival Speaks

We have used this idea many times in our presentations, videos and church meetings and have found it to have a great effect on those listening. It brings the state of our nation to our attention and shows that we, as Christians, have a responsibility to pray and see things change. Rather than just 'speaking out' information on the nation, it is portrayed in a way that people can use their ears and eyes to hear and see for themselves what the situation is like. When people see it for themselves, they develop more of a hunger to pray.

This idea is probably more suited to a large audience than a small group, but it can be adapted for use in a home.

THE PREPARATION

You will need to pick three or four people to portray what the nation is like. Choose people who have been trained in speech and drama if possible, but if not then choose those who have a good clear voice and a good imagination. Give them their scripts long before the event so that they can practise beforehand and make sure you have a rehearsal of all the 'voices' before the event starts. I have used stories from people we have met and touched with the message of Jesus and have just changed their names to protect them. However, you can use other people's stories if you prefer.

If at all possible, it will be helpful to use lighting effects as described below. Go through this with the person in charge of the lighting.

You will need to display the statistics mentioned below on overhead or video screens.

Be ready to lead your audience into a time of intercession after the presentation.

Ask your worship band or leader to be ready to lead people in the song 'Heal our nation' (*Songs of Fellowship* No. 365).

THE IDEA

You can use this idea as part of a presentation or as an introduction to a night of prayer and intercession.

At the beginning of your event, invite the audience or group to come with you on a journey to discover what your nation is like. Encourage them to listen to the audible voices they will hear, but also to open their ears to hear God's heart for their nation. Darken the room and have your 'readers' come on stage (or into the room) without the audience seeing them. One by one they should come to the microphone and read their 'story'. Make sure the lighting is sufficient for them to be able to see what they are reading, but dark enough so that nobody can see their face. They should read the script as though the person were them.

Person number 1

I can't bear to look at myself in the mirror. I think I look ugly and disgusting. My parents are divorced and it has made me feel that I am a bit of rubbish that has been thrown on the floor. I don't have any friends and there is no one I can trust – least of all my parents. No one cares about me. What is love all about? I tell you, in my world love just does not exist.

Person number 2

Hi, my name is Mark and I am eleven years old. I got thrown out of my home last year and told never to come back again. I eventually got put in a children's home, but I have run away so many times. I hate it. I prefer to live on the streets. There's no one to tell me what to do then. At times I feel really lonely, but I would never tell anyone that – they'd think I'd gone soft. Drugs are my only friends. I feel good when I take drugs – it numbs the pain in me.

Person number 3

Hi, my name is Suzy and I hate everyone. I can't believe God would ever love me. The only love I have received has been from my cat. My father said he loved me and ended up abusing me sexually and physically. I will never forgive him. I hate the very road he walks on. He can burn in hell for all I care. The hurt and pain in me will never go away. No one can help me – I'm beyond help.

Person number 4

Hi, I'm Peter and I live in the north of England. I've had three dads. My first dad physically abused me and my mum when he got drunk each night. I was so scared of him and life was awful while he was around, but eventually my mum divorced him and things were all right for a while. But then my mum married again and my second dad used to abuse me too – only this time he not only physically abused me but sexually abused me too. I didn't know what to do as I knew my mum would not believe what was happening to me. Eventually, my mum and my second dad separated and things were OK for a while. However, it wasn't long before my mum invited my third dad to live with her. He just didn't want me and told my mum that she had to put me in a children's home. I have been living there ever since. The only friends I have are the ones I have made at school. One day, we decided to do a séance just for a bit of fun, but things started to go wrong. The television exploded and I started to have dreams, which then began to come true. I dreamt that my cousin got hurt and the next day my cousin got hurt. I then dreamt that there would be a motorway disaster and then in the next week there was a major motorway disaster. I am so scared. I don't want to go to sleep at night in case I dream something that comes true the following day. What can I do? Can anybody help me?

After all your readers have finished, arrange for the worship band to start playing 'Heal our nation' – instrumental only in the background – while you put the statistics of the nation on the video or overhead screen. I have given some statistics below that you can use, or you can research some statistics yourself.

At least one child dies every week following abuse or neglect. (NSPCC)

Around 2 million children see their GP each year for emotional and psychological problems. (Tim Field, *Bullycide: Death at Playtime*)

Around a third of all 16–26-year-olds have taken an illegal drug. (*The Guardian*, June 2000)

Every year in England and Wales over 19,000 young men attempt suicide – one every half an hour. (The Samaritans)

In Britain, 3,700 girls under the age of 16 have babies each year. We have the highest teenage pregnancy and abortion rates in Europe. (*Sunday Mirror*, 2000)

A million young people left the church in the 1990s.

After the statistics have been shown, ask the band to lead everyone in the song 'Heal our Nation', encouraging them to make it their prayer to God for the nation they live in.

Heal our Nation

Lord, we long for you to move in power.
There's a hunger deep within our hearts
To see healing in our nation.
Send your Spirit to revive us.

Heal our nation,
Heal our nation,
Heal our nation.
Pour out your Spirit on this land.

Lord, we hear your Spirit coming closer,
A mighty wave to break upon our land.
Bring justice and forgiveness.
God, we cry to you 'Revive us!'

Trish Morgan/Ray Goudie/Ian Townend/Dave Bankhead
Copyright © Thankyou Music 1986. Used by permission

After this enter into a time of intercession. You may wish everyone to cry out to God at the same time. Alternatively, people could come to the front one by one and pray through the microphone. Another option is to get them into small groups to pray. Whichever you do, encourage them to use the information they have been given to pray like they have never prayed before.

You may wish to stop the intercession midway and get some people to give testimonies of how they have been saved by the power of God. Perhaps some people may have come from hopeless situations and God came into their lives and saved them. With each testimony, God will plant faith in people's hearts to believe that the same can happen in their family, neighbourhood, town, city or nation.

29 The Word Speaks

So many of us do not see ourselves as God sees us, and this idea brings home to people just how precious we are in God's sight. Many people have been encouraged and inspired through hearing God as they meditated on God's word.

THE PREPARATION

Arrange to have Isaiah 43:1 displayed on the overhead or video screen. If this is not possible, write it on a flip chart or have it printed on paper so that each person has a copy of the verse.

> *This is what the Lord says – he who created you . . . he who formed you . . . 'Fear not, for I have redeemed you . . . by name; you are mine.' (Isaiah 43:1)*

You will also need to arrange for track 5 to be played of my recording *A God Encounter* or play track 10 of the same CD and ask someone with a clear voice to read the paraphrase of the creation story.

THE IDEA

This idea gets people to think about how wonderfully we have been made and how God looked at his creation and said, 'This is very good.' Tell people that you are going to listen to a paraphrased reading of Genesis 1. Explain to them that all they need to do for this form of meditation is to find a space on the floor, relax and allow their thoughts to take in what they hear. Explain that after the first form of meditation, you will then go into a form of biblical meditation, which will be displayed on the video or overhead screen. Alternatively, people could look up the verse in their Bibles.

Make sure you explain before you begin how to meditate (see Idea 23 for details). It would be good to go through this with people just in case they do not know how to meditate. Explain that at the end of the two meditations you will be asking for some volunteers to come up to the front and say what they received from God.

Play track 5 of *A God Encounter*, or ask your prearranged person to come and read the following over track 10.

You Are 'Very' Good

Come with me back before time began – when empty darkness covered the face of the earth. The earth was a shapeless chaotic mess – formless and empty. Breaking into this dark shapeless formless mess comes the Word. Like a sharp blade cutting through ice, the Word speaks; 'Let there be light' and light appears. The light and darkness took it in turn to rule and together they formed the first day. And the Word was delighted and rejoiced in what he had made and said, 'This is good.'

The Word again spoke: 'Let the vapours separate to form the sky above and the oceans below.' And it was so: the Word observed what he had made and said, 'This is good!'

The Word spoke to the waters: 'Give way. Be gathered into one place and let the earth be seen.' Then the Word spoke to the earth: 'Produce vegetation – trees, grass, plants and fruit of all kinds.' And it happened just as he said. And the Word looked and said, 'This is good.'

The Word spoke: 'Let bright lights appear in the sky and give light to the earth and to identify day and night.' The Word made the sun, the moon and the stars to give light on the earth. And the

Word was pleased with what he had made and said, 'This is good.'

The Word spoke to the waters to produce fish and all kinds of living creatures, and it was so. The Word spoke and the skies were filled with birds of every kind. The Word looked at them with pleasure, blessed them and told them, 'Multiply – let your numbers increase. Fill the earth.' And the Word said, 'This is good.'

The Word spoke and the land produced every kind of animal, cattle, reptiles, wild creatures, wildlife of every kind. The Word saw what he had made and said, 'This is good.'

The Word then said, 'Let mankind be made in the image of God, to rule over the earth, the skies and the seas.' So the Word created male and female in the image of himself. The Word breathed into mankind the breath of life and blessed them. 'Be fruitful and increase in number – fill the earth. Rule over the fish of the seas, the birds of the skies and every living creature that moves.' The Word looked and danced and rejoiced in what he had made and said, 'This is very good.'

Now hear the word of God speak deep into your own heart. As God looks at you he says, 'You are very good. You are special in my sight. I have made you in my image and I am pleased with what I have made.' Open up your heart and allow God's word to penetrate your whole being as God says to you, 'You are very good.'

Once this is read, let the music run for a few more minutes to allow people time to digest what God is saying, then at an appropriate point ask people to enter into the second meditation. Put Isaiah 43:1 on the overhead or video screen (or hand out your printed paper if it is a small group). Keep the music playing during the second form of meditation and then after a few minutes ask for volunteers to share what they received from God.

30 Prayer Speaks

My husband Ray used to be the drummer in a band we founded in the 1980s called Heartbeat, so this idea is particularly close to his heart. We have sixteen or so drummers (or ex-drummers) in NGM, which is helpful when it comes to this idea.

THE PREPARATION

If you have any drummers in your church or group, arrange for several drums or percussion instruments to be set up at various points around the venue. But do make sure the drummers can drum and not just make a noise. There is a difference! The best drums to use for this are toms, congas, etc.

Arrange for certain musicians to bring their instruments for this idea. Pick good musicians who you know will be able to enter into this idea and lead worship sensitively.

If you are using this idea in a small group, it may be wise to go to your church building rather than meet in your home, where it may cause problems with your neighbours.

Choose your subjects for intercession and make sure you have all the information needed so that you can all pray intelligently about each subject.

Do not use chairs at the venue unless it is absolutely necessary, and make sure you have a microphone, because you will need it to be heard above the drumming and the intercession.

THE IDEA

This idea provides an opportunity for people to get fully involved in the worship and intercession.

At the beginning of your event, explain that you would like everyone to enter into a time of intercession together on various subjects. However, instead of getting into small groups to pray, encourage everyone to get involved in praying by using whatever gifts they have: the dancers could dance their intercession, the singers could sing out their prayers, and those who have instruments could pray and prophesy through their instrument. Encourage everyone to pray and to reach out to God for scriptures they could read.

Explain that the reason why there are few chairs around is because you want to give room for each person to move around or dance as they pray.

After your explanations, the first subject should be announced, along with information on that subject so that people are fully aware of what they are praying for. Then ask the drummers to start drumming, prophetically calling the people to pray. As they are beginning to drum, encourage people to start to pray out loud to God. When the drummers begin to fade, encourage people to start to come to the microphone to pray, read the Bible, prophesy or intercede through an instrument (e.g. violin, sax, guitar). Encourage the dancers to come and dance their prayer. Work very closely with your worship leader, making sure that they lead people in worship at the right time. Encourage creativity but also make sure everything is done correctly and in order.

Continue until you feel that the subject has been exhausted and then move on to the second subject for intercession.

Sight

31 See the Word

I believe it is so important for us as Christians to have the word of God within us, and the best way of doing that is to memorise portions of the Bible. When I was young, my parents encouraged me to memorise the Bible and I am enormously grateful for that. However, this no longer seems to be common practice. I believe it is vital that we teach and encourage each other to hide the word of God in our hearts, and memorising is a great way of doing just that. This idea will show people that memorising together, rather than on an individual basis, can be fun.

THE PREPARATION

If you are able, display the various verses and reasons for memorising as mentioned below on the overhead or video screen. If you are using this idea in a home and do not have facilities for overhead or video, have the verses printed out on paper or make sure everyone brings a NIV Bible. Likewise, you could print out the 'Reasons for memorising Scripture' below, or alternatively you could purchase a copy of my book *Nancy Goudie's Spiritual Health Workout* for everyone in your group. The reasons for memorising are given in this book. It will also give you many different and creative exercises to do together.

If you are using music to help you memorise then I would recommend you use a track with no lyrics and a steady beat.

Do rehearse the verse with the music beforehand so that you are familiar with the process.

THE IDEA

It is good at the beginning, before you move into the actual memorising, to explain what you are going to do and why. It is important to let people know that memorising can be fun because most people will envisage it being hard work and something to be avoided. People may think that their memory is so bad that there is no point in them joining in, so encourage them by telling them that each person's memory, whether good or bad, can be trained. It may surprise people to know that exercise is very good for your memory. If you continue to exercise your memory, it will improve. What better way to improve your memory than to fill it with the Bible?

Explain that there are many reasons why we should memorise Scripture, and take time to go through each one. I have given you four reasons, but you may wish to use your own biblical reasons why we should memorise.

Reasons for memorising Scripture

1. God has told us to do so (Deuteronomy 11:18).
2. It helps in moments of weakness or temptation; for example when the enemy tempts Jesus, he fights back by quoting Scripture (Matthew 4:4).
3. It is really helpful when we are sharing our faith with others. Hebrews 4:12 says that God's word is sharper than a two-edged sword.
4. It is really helpful in finding God's direction and guidance for our lives (Proverbs 3:1–6).

How to memorise Scripture

Explain that the best way to memorise Scripture is to break the verse into portions. Using 1 Thessalonians 5:16–18 as an example, I would encourage people to learn the first section first: *Be joyful always.* The best way to do this is to say it over and over again until you think you have got it in your mind. Then add the second section to it and say them together: *Be joyful always; pray continually.* Do this until you feel you have memorised them. Then repeat the same process adding the third section: *Be joyful always; pray continually; give thanks in all circumstances*, before adding the fourth and repeating the same process until you are able to say it completely.

It is helpful to memorise to music. Most people know worship songs not because they have consciously tried to memorise them but because they have learned them to music. The use of music and rhythm helps our memory banks to retain the information received. Let people know that you are going to use these two methods of memorising in the next few minutes.

If you are able, display Galatians 2:20 on the overhead or video screen. If you are in a home and cannot use overhead facilities, have the verse printed out on paper or ask people to follow it in their Bible. Show them that the verse splits into five portions:

First portion: *I have been crucified with Christ*
Second portion: *and I no longer live*
Third portion: *but Christ lives in me.*
                 (When it comes to this line let people know that you are going to say this bit twice, i.e. *but Christ lives in me, but Christ lives in me.*)
Fourth portion: *The life I live in the body, I live by faith in the Son of God*
Fifth portion: *who loved me and gave himself for me.*

At this point make sure everyone knows what they are doing and understands how to memorise. Then use a CD/cassette player to play the music. Wait until the beat starts and then encourage everyone to join with you in memorising this verse. Do remember to rehearse this before teaching others.

Repeat the first portion over and over again, perhaps four times, before adding the second section. Once you feel you have learned these two, add the third section and so on until you reach the end of the verse. Once you have said it all the way through, stop the music and start again at the beginning. Then together, learn the whole verse all the way through until the end of the track. When you have gone through it, give people five minutes or so to review what they have just learned. Then ask for volunteers to come up to the front and say it to the music. You can add an element of fun to the exercise by asking your volunteers to dance to the music as well as saying the memory verse. To encourage people to volunteer have a prize for each person who tries to say the verse and a bigger prize for the person who performs it best.

Always make sure you tell people at the end that the test as to whether or not they have memorised the verse will be if they can still say it in six months' time. You can encourage memorising by revising the verse or verses publicly together each time you meet. Another way of encouraging individuals to memorise is to give them little cards or paper with the verse or verses printed on them and ask them to place the card or paper where they will see it every day. Ask them to duplicate the verse and put it in several places – on their dressing table, in their car, in their diary, on their desk at work, etc. When they see the verse it will remind them to continue to memorise it.

32 See the Bins

This idea is particularly effective in young people's evangelistic meetings. We have found that God uses it to release many from drugs, alcohol, sex, cigarettes, etc.

THE PREPARATION

You will need one or two large dustbins, depending on the size of your outreach event. Place the bins at the front of the hall, one on either side of the platform or stage, within easy reach of the audience but within sight of the leader of the event. Arrange for two responsible people in leadership to empty the bins at the end of the evening.

If you are using this idea in your home as an evangelistic event for young people, make sure the bins are placed in easy reach of everyone, but do keep an eye on them because you don't want items thrown in the bins to be retrieved by others.

THE IDEA

At an appropriate time in your outreach event, bring the bins to the attention of your group. Let them know that they are there so that they can throw away their drugs, cigarettes or anything else that will hinder them from becoming close to God. If you are having a message or a challenging talk, bring the bins to their attention again and ask them to come to the front and throw in the bin anything that would stop them from becoming close to God or becoming God's friend. You

can either encourage people to do this throughout the night
or have an appeal at some point. Anytime we have used this,
we have found many coming to know the Lord and all sorts
of things in the bins.

33 See the Picture

This is a very effective way of complementing the talk in a main meeting event. I have used this many times in my Spiritual Health Weekends with encouraging results.

The first time we used this idea was many years ago when Ray and I were in a band called Unity. Our sister-in-law, Shiona Goudie, was very good at art, so Derek, Ray's brother, and Ray asked Shiona to paint a picture of Jesus during one of Unity's performances. We found it was a very powerful way of portraying the message of Jesus.

THE PREPARATION

You will need to find out if you have any creative artists in your church or circle of friends. Meet with them beforehand and explain what you are speaking on and what you would like them to do throughout the meeting. Let them know how long you or the preacher is speaking for.

Arrange for the artist to set up prior to the start of the event, preferably on the stage or platform. Make sure that the audience has a clear view of the picture being painted.

THE IDEA

Bring the artist to the people's attention before the talk starts otherwise they will be a distraction to what is being said. Let people know that the artist is going to paint as you speak and at the end of the meeting they will have drawn something that will reflect what you are saying.

If you wish, and if the artist agrees, you can give the painting away at the end of the meeting. Anytime we have used this idea, several people have wanted to have the painting at the end. Not only is it a nice painting, but it also reminds them of what God said to them during the meeting.

34 See the Funeral

We first used this idea, which is based on Colossians 3:5, at a Kingdom Faith camp in the 1980s. It is a brilliant way of allowing people to see what we must do to the old sinful nature.

THE PREPARATION

You will need an oblong-shaped box made to look like a coffin. Place this at the side of the stage or platform.

Have some paper and pens ready in case people need them.

If you are able, display Romans 6:6–11 on the overhead or video screen.

If you are using this idea in a home, have the verse printed out on paper or make sure you have enough Bibles so that people can look up the verse. It would also perhaps be appropriate to scale the 'coffin' down and have just a small box in the room with you.

THE IDEA

At an appropriate place in your meeting/event, let people know that you are going to hold a funeral service. Read Colossians 3:1–10. Bring to their attention the fact that you have a coffin present, but instead of burying a person, everyone is being encouraged to bury their 'old nature'. At an appropriate time, possibly after the talk, ask people to write down on a piece of paper the things in their lives they would like to bury, such as pride, selfishness, greed, sexual sins, drugs, excess alcohol or cigarettes. They should write each thing down as God highlights it. Then ask them to file past the coffin one by one and put their piece of paper in the coffin as a declaration that the old self has been put to death.

After this has been done, display Romans 6:6–11 on the overhead or video screen, or hand out the verse printed on paper, or ask the group to look up the reference in their Bibles. Say it together out loud. This should be followed by a time of praise, celebrating that the old life has gone and the new has come. Make sure you have a time when some people can come for counselling if they feel they would like someone to pray with them specifically about the things God highlighted during the evening.

35 See the Breakthrough

I first came across this idea when I went to hear Ed Silvoso speak at Birmingham many years ago, and since then we have used it as a method of prayer. I have also used it at my Spiritual Health conferences and have had many letters from people telling me how much God spoke to them through this method of intercession.

The idea is based on the principle that if you keep hitting or 'bashing' at one spot on a brick wall, even though the brick wall is thick and it doesn't seem as though you are getting anywhere, if you keep knocking at the same spot eventually you will have a breakthrough.

THE PREPARATION

You will need to ask God for a verse to use as the 'bash' verse. Pick one that is easy to memorise and isn't too long. Depending on the size of your group, you can either have the verse written on small pieces of paper so that people can take them home with them to stick on their fridge, in their car, or keep in their Bible, or encourage people to write it out for themselves.

If you are able, display your chosen verse on the overhead or video screen too.

THE IDEA

The idea is to ask people to use a 'bash' verse to intercede for a specific purpose. You may wish to intercede for a breakthrough to happen in your area, town or city, or for a breakthrough to take place in your own lives. One of the verses we have used in the past is Isaiah 44:3: 'For I will pour water on the thirsty land, and streams on the dry ground; I will pour out my Spirit on your offspring, and my blessing on your descendants.' Ask people to use this verse in prayer every day – to say it out loud to God as many times as it comes to their mind. Encourage them to display the verse in several places where they will see it during the day and pray it into being each time they see it.

Ask people to memorise the verse. Explain to them that the best way of memorising is to break the verse into small portions. Then take the first portion and learn that part first. Once you have learned that, then add the second portion to it and learn the first and second portions together and so on throughout the verse (see Idea 31).

If you wish, you can ask a few people to come to the front and show that they have been able to memorise the verse. Encourage people to use this verse to see God move in their community, their neighbourhood, their friends' lives or their families. Encourage them to go through the verse bit by bit, asking God to pour water on the thirsty land, etc. Ask them to meditate on the verse, to paraphrase it, to memorise it and to pray it out over and over again, believing God for a great breakthrough. We usually use a verse like this for forty days, but you can choose to pray it out for longer or shorter, depending on your circumstances. Encourage people to keep on 'bashing' until they see a breakthrough in their own life or in the lives or others.

When we have used this method of praying, significant things have happened and God has answered our prayers in amazing ways, so have a great 'bash'!

36 See the Breath

I recently used this idea when speaking at an international conference. It enabled people to 'see' what God wanted to do in their own nation and to begin to pray it into existence.

THE PREPARATION

You will need to arrange for someone who is used to speaking and who has a clear strong voice to read the 'Come – Breath of God' script given below. When choosing your reader, bear in mind that some of the script needs to be preached rather than just spoken. Alternatively, you could use my recording *A God Encounter*, track 4.

This idea can also be used for a small group situation. However, in that case it might be better to use the recording rather than ask someone to read the script.

THE IDEA

At the beginning of the meeting, lay the foundation for what you want to do through the reading of Scripture and prayer. Explain to people that you are going to use Scripture and the spoken word to pray for your nation, city, town or whatever. If you are asking someone to read the script below, play track 9 of my recording *A God Encounter* in the background.

Come – Breath of God

Travel with me back in time to where God spoke to the prophet Ezekiel. I want you to imagine that you are Ezekiel and that this is happening to you.

The hand of the Lord was upon me, and he brought me out by the Spirit of the Lord and set me in the middle of a valley; it was full of bones. He led me back and forth among them, and I saw a great many bones on the floor of the valley, bones that were very dry. He asked me, 'Son of man, can these bones live?' I said, 'O Sovereign Lord, you alone know.'

Look at the valley and the dry bones. Keeping that image in your mind, now picture your street, your town, your city, the schools, colleges, your work place, the media and any other areas that God shows you. And as you look, hear the word of God again: 'Son of man, can these bones live?'

'Then he said to me, "Prophesy to these bones and say to them, 'Dry bones, hear the word of the Lord! This is what the Sovereign Lord says to these bones: I will make breath enter you, and you will come to life. I will attach tendons to you and make flesh come upon you and cover you with skin; I will put breath in you, and you will come to life. Then you will know that I am the Lord.'"'

I want you to imagine the breath of God coming upon all the areas God showed you – your street, your town, your city, your schools, colleges, your work place, the media. See the breath and the presence of God entering into these places – see it in your mind. Use your imagination. Ask God to increase your faith.

'So I prophesied as I was commanded. And as I was prophesying, there was a noise, a rattling sound, and the bones came together, bone to bone. I looked, and tendons and flesh appeared on them and skin covered them, but there was no breath in them. Then he said to me, "Prophesy to the breath; prophesy, son of man, and say to it, 'This is what the Sovereign

Lord says: Come from the four winds, O breath, and breathe into these slain, that they may live.' " So I prophesied as I was commanded, and breath entered into them; they came to life and stood up on their feet – a vast army.'

Listen – can you hear the rattling? Supernatural sounds and signs of God moving across the world. Can you hear the noise as the bones come together in all the different areas? Think of all the people you know. See them rising up as a radical vast new mission army. Can you hear the sound of marching? Can you see them from every tribe and nation marching together as one for the kingdom?

'Then he said to me: "Son of man, these bones are the whole house of Israel. They say, 'Our bones are dried up and our hope is gone; we are cut off.' Therefore prophesy to them: 'This is what the Sovereign Lord says: O my people, I am going to open your graves and bring you up from them . . . I will put my Spirit in you and you will live, and I will settle you in your own land. Then you will know that I the Lord have spoken, and I have done it, declares the Lord.' "'

Now speak out these words of life and hope over all the 'dry bones' that you know across the world. Use your imagination and your faith to believe God for his breath to enter your street, your town, your city, your nation, and all the other areas God showed you during this meditation.

37 See Joshua

We have used this idea, which is based on Joshua 6:1–20, many times to teach about the importance of obedience to God, intercession and faith in God and our leaders. It is a very practical and creative way of discovering these truths for ourselves.

THE PREPARATION

Read Joshua 6:1–20 so that you are aware of the story in detail.

You will need four or five chairs in the middle of your room that you can call Jericho. Depending on the size of your group, make 'Jericho' big enough for people to march round.

THE IDEA

Read Joshua 6:1–20 to your group. Explain to them that you are going to use this story to illustrate the importance of being obedient to God in every situation, and say that each person in the event will be involved in a huge drama. Ask for seven volunteers to become the seven priests mentioned in verse 6. Explain that they will go at the end of the people and they are to pretend that they have trumpets. Ask for volunteers to become the armed guard who will march in front of the ark of the Lord's covenant and for others to be the rear guard who follow behind the ark, as mentioned in verse 9.

Ask for three or four volunteers to be the residents of

Jericho. When the army marches round Jericho, they have to taunt the Israelites, saying things like, 'What do you think you're doing? You mean to tell me that God told you to do this! You will never have victory doing that! You all look so stupid. You say you are trusting God – well are you still going to trust him when you are defeated?' Ask them to stand on the chairs you have laid out.

Appoint someone to be Joshua. Explain that God has told Joshua that all of you should march round the walls of Jericho with the priests blowing their trumpets. Ask the rest of the congregation to get into pairs behind the rear guard.

The first day begins. Joshua commands the people to go round the walls of Jericho once and then return to camp. The guards lead the way round Jericho with the seven priests following, and as they do, they blow their trumpets. If you have anyone in your group who can play the trumpet, tell them that this is their big moment! However, as it is more likely that you won't know anyone who can get a sound out of a trumpet never mind play it, ask the 'priests' to pretend they have trumpets and get them to make the noise with their mouths.

Then comes the ark. Have four or six people pretending to carry the ark of the covenant, followed by the rear guard. Following them, in silence, are the people of Israel. (Make sure that even when the people on the walls of Jericho taunt them, they do not respond in any way at all. They must keep silent.)

When they return to camp, get the people to sit on the floor and ask them to think how they might have felt towards Joshua, their leaders or even God. Although it does not say this in the Bible, I'm sure some people might have said, 'Does Joshua really know what he is doing?' 'Did he really hear from God?' 'This is ridiculous – we need to fight, not walk round the walls in silence.' Get the people to moan and groan to Joshua, among themselves and also to God.

A few minutes later, announce to your group that it is now the second day and ask them to repeat what they did the previous day and again to moan when they get back to base. Continue this way until you get to the seventh day. Remind the 'taunters' to keep their comments coming and to make them relevant to faith projects and church vision today, as well as to the story in Joshua.

On the seventh day, Joshua should explain that today the people are not going to march round the city once, but they are going to march round it seven times. He should tell them that when they circle the city they must keep silent as they did before, with only the trumpets sounding from the priests. However, after they have circled the city seven times and after Joshua has said, 'Shout! For the Lord has given you the city!' the people should all give a huge shout.

Get them to imagine that the walls have fallen down and to rush in and grab hold of the people who have been taunting them.

When the whole story is complete, explain in full the following points:

1. The importance of obeying God even when his instructions seem unreasonable
2. The importance of trusting our leaders. Joshua was the one God met and spoke to. The children of Israel needed to put their trust not only in God, but also in Joshua, their leader. It wasn't long since Moses had died and it would have been easy for people to question whether Joshua had heard from God correctly.
3. The children of Israel must have thought that by 'walking' they were not accomplishing much, but by being obedient to God their 'walking' became intercession.
4. The importance of not listening to the enemy's voice in our daily walk. If they had listened to the people on top of the wall they would never have seen their miracle take

place. The taunting seemed to have a ring of truth about it, but in actual fact the taunting was lies!

5. The importance of following God even when you have never been that way before. God had never asked the children of Israel to walk round a city in silence before. It would have been easy to say, 'This is different. I don't like this. It doesn't seem like something God would say.' Emphasise that being intimate with God is so important.

As I am sure you can see, this is an excellent way of showing people just how important these points are in our daily walk with God.

38 See Daniel

We have used this idea many times to bring home what
happens when you intercede. It explains the importance of
intercession and what happens in spiritual warfare.

THE PREPARATION

You will need a thick rope long enough for a tug of war. You
will also need to read Daniel 9 so that you are aware of the
story.

Ask four of your leaders to help you in the organising of
this drama sketch and arrange for them to read through the
instructions listed below before the event.

THE IDEA

Read Daniel 9 to your group and explain that you are all
going to be involved in a sketch, which is based on this story.

Divide your group into four. One group should be called
the 'church', another group called the 'world', another
group 'the angels' and another 'the demonic realm'. Appoint
a leader to each group and ask the four leaders to go through
the following points with their group.

The church

Set aside from this group two women whose role will be to
stand in the corner of their group interceding and praying
out loud to God for the world to come to know him. Point
out the reason that you have chosen two women is that,

today, it is often the women who are faithful in intercession.
The rest need to compile on a piece of paper a list of atti-
tudes that sometimes we see displayed in the church, for
example apathy, too busy watching TV, etc.

Explain that as the intercessors pray and as the angels
shout words of encouragement to the church, more of the
church leave their apathy behind and join the intercessors'
group and begin to pray for the lost. As they do, more of the
world join the church. At the end of the sketch, most of the
church should be praying, but there will be a few who are still
apathetic towards it.

The world

Ask the world to compile a list of things to shout to the
church, like, 'You're not relevant'; 'I don't need to respond
to God now'; 'You're boring!'; 'I don't want to go to church
and listen to folk music'.

Explain that slowly, as the intercessors' group increases,
people move from this group to the church group, but that
at the end there will still be some people left in the world
group.

The angels

A few of the angels are to be on one side of the tug of war
rope – and as the church responds to the call to pray, more
angels are added. At the beginning of the tug of war, the
angels need to be seen to be losing, but at the end, when more
people are praying, the angels start to win the battle.

Ask the angels to compile a list of things to shout to the
church at the appropriate time, like 'Come on, church,
pray!'; 'Stop watching so much TV and start praying', etc.
They also need to compile a list of things to shout to the
unchurched, like 'Respond to Jesus now'; 'Let him take
control of your life', etc.

The demonic realm

Some of this group need to be on the other end of the tug of war rope. At the beginning they are winning, but as more angels are added to the other side, they begin to lose. Do make sure that everyone involved in the tug of war knows that although it can get 'rough', they must not lose sight of what it is all about.

This group needs to compile two lists of shouts: one to the church saying things like, 'Be apathetic', and the other to the unchurched saying things like, 'Put it off – you don't need to come to know Jesus yet.'

Give each group time to ask questions of their leader and only continue when people have compiled their lists and understand what is required of them.

When everyone is ready, start with the demonic realm group and ask them what they are shouting to the world. Get them to shout out their list. Then ask them to shout what they are saying to the church.

Then ask the angel group what they are saying to the world and get them to shout it out. Then ask them to shout out what they are saying to the church group.

Get the world to shout to the church the items from their list, then ask the church to shout their comments to the world.

Remind them that as they are shouting, the tug of war between good and evil will be happening. You will need to keep the whole thing moving and make sure it's done properly and according to plan. The sketch finishes when the angels win the tug of war.

At the end, go through exactly what was happening. Explain that as the intercessors prayed, things changed and more people became Christians. As the prayers went up, more angels were released into the battle against the enemy and they were able eventually to win the battle. Point out that more people from the church joined the intercessors' group, but not all did. Many became Christians from the world group, but again not everyone did. Bring out the point of how important it is to have people praying, and to be listening to the voice of God and not the voice of self or the enemy. Encourage people in their own prayer life to be part of that prayer army whose prayers are winning the battles in the heavenlies.

It may be good to get people into groups to discuss how they can put prayer as a higher priority in their own lives and in the life of the church. A couple of things we did as a church and community was to install a prayer room in our complex where people could go and pray to God at any time. The prayer room has been set up so that it is easy for people to pray and sense God's presence. To see the kind of things we have done, visit our NGM website at www.ngm.org.uk Another way to get involved in more prayer might be to get your church or group involved in 24/7 prayer. For information on 24/7 prayer visit their website at www.24/7prayer.com

You can then start to intercede for the items you feel are the key issues for your church, community, nation or whatever.

39 See the Prayers

This is a great idea to use if you are keen to see your congregation, cell or small group grow in the desire to pray. Often through showing people how to do it and how to do it creatively can release them into depths of prayer they have never experienced before.

THE PREPARATION

If you can, prepare several overheads (see below for details). You will also need to ask your worship leader or band to lead through the music and to be able to sing/play 'The great awakening' (*Songs of Fellowship 2* 'Lord pour out Your Spirit') or another suitable song. If you are unable to use overhead or video facilities because you are in a home or because you don't have access to this type of equipment, read out the verses as you come to them and ask people to look them up in their Bibles, or have the verses and the information printed out on paper.

You will also need to prepare three places in your venue (probably using the corners of the room) with a huge sheet of white paper on a flip chart or on the wall and lots of pens. One area will be called 'Your family life' one will be called 'Your business/education life' and the third will be called 'Your social life'. Display those titles beside each area. Put up posters on the wall that represent each name, for example display photos of business people or schools. If you are using this idea in a home, you may wish to use a different room for each area.

If possible, have some matches and a large candle near you so that you can light it when applicable.

Display a poster that says 'Never give up!' (or put this on the overhead or video screen at the appropriate time).

THE IDEA

At the beginning display on your overhead or video screen Luke 11:1: 'One day Jesus was praying in a certain place. When he finished, one of his disciples said to him, "Lord, teach us to pray."' I am amazed when I read that verse that the disciples asked Jesus to teach them how to pray, because the Jews were always a nation that had been taught from their earliest days that they should pray to God. Suggest to people that there must have been something different about Jesus' prayers that inspired them. Explain that you are going to look at some of the ways Jesus prayed and then do the same.

Display the following information on the overhead or video screen, or have it on printed sheets so that each person can have one.

Ways that Jesus Prayed

1. He prayed out loud.
2. He was intimate.
3. He prayed anywhere.
4. He was specific.
5. He was persistent.
6. He prayed in faith.
7. He prayed with others.
8. He submitted to his Father's will.

Then look in detail at each of the ways Jesus prayed.

1. He prayed out loud

I'm sure there will be some in your group who do not speak
out their prayers but instead 'think' their prayers. As I travel
I am always amazed at how many people think their prayers.
Although there is nothing wrong with people thinking their
prayers, if they do, it can often lead to wandering thoughts,
whereas speaking their prayers will help them to focus much
better. It will also encourage them to pray in public more
often because they will be used to the sound of their own
voice in prayer.

2. He was intimate

Jesus spoke to God as if he really knew him and even called
him Daddy. He didn't feel he needed to use old-fashioned
language with God but instead spoke to him as he would a
friend. Jesus had such an intimate relationship with God and
the great news for us is that God wants to have that kind of
relationship with us. It is important for us to develop our
relationship with God and really know him. It is not sufficient just to know *about* him – we must know him intimately.
That means we can share our deepest desires and secrets with
him and also it means that God will be able to share his
heart, plans and secrets with us. Explain that growing in intimacy with God will change your whole life.

3. He prayed anywhere

No matter where Jesus was he prayed. This is an exercise for
us all to develop. So many times people only remember to
pray when a problem arises, but we need to be people who
bring God into our lives twenty-four hours a day. Encourage
people to pray at any time, no matter where they are.

4. He was specific

If you look at Jesus' prayers in the Bible you will discover
that he was specific. So often when we come to God in prayer

we just say, 'God bless so and so,' instead of telling God in which way we would like that person to be blessed.

5. He was persistent

Mark 8:22–25 tells us the story of Jesus praying for a blind man. When the blind man is not healed completely, Jesus prays a second time for the man to be healed. In other words, Jesus was persistent in his prayers. Jesus also teaches us in Luke 11:5–10 and Luke 18:1–8 to be persistent in our prayers and not to give up.

6. He prayed in faith

In Mark 11:22–24 Jesus encourages us to have faith in God and to continue to display that faith when we pray. I also believe that there is little point in praying for something specific to happen if we pray without any expectation that God will do what we ask. Explain to your group that today you are going to ask God to increase your faith in him.

7. He prayed with others

This is something that many of your group may be doing already, but it is important to remember the promise that Jesus spoke about in Matthew 18:19–20.

It might also be good to emphasise the importance of married couples praying together. With so many marriages breaking up, if couples pray together it can help to bring them closer to each other and closer to God.

8. He submitted to his Father's will

Jesus always willingly submitted to his Father's will. In Luke 22:42 he prayed to his Father in heaven and said, 'Father, if you are willing, take this cup from me; yet not my will, but yours be done.' In John 4:34 Jesus states quite clearly: 'My food . . . is to do the will of him who sent me and to finish his work.'

After going through this list, explain to people that you are going to enter into a time of prayer using all these ways that Jesus prayed. You are going to pray about your nation, your city or town, your friends through the song 'The great awakening'.

Display the words given below on your video or overhead screen and ask your worship leader or band to play this song. Encourage people to pray as they sing. Again, if you have no overhead or video facilities, print the song out on paper so that each person can have a copy. Alternatively, rather than singing, you could listen to the song being played by the worship band or to a recording of it.

The Great Awakening

Lord, pour out your Spirit
On all the peoples of the earth.
Let your sons and daughters
Speak your words of prophecy.
Send us dreams and visions,
Reveal the secrets of your heart.
Lord, our faith is rising
Let all Heaven sound the coming of your day.

There's gonna be a great awakening,
There's gonna be a great revival in our land.
There's gonna be a great awakening,
And everyone who calls on Jesus they will be saved.

Lord, pour out your Spirit
On all the nations of the world.
Let them see your glory,
Let them fall in reverent awe.
Show your mighty power,
Shake the heavens and the earth.

Lord, the world is waiting,
Let creation see the coming of your day.

1. He prayed out loud

After you have sung the song a couple of times, while the band is still playing the song, encourage people to speak out their prayers together. Tell them not to worry about what their neighbour is thinking or doing, but instead to concentrate on their own prayers to God for revival. Encourage them to pray for their unsaved family, friends or neighbours and perhaps use the second verse of the song to help them in their prayers. Allow this to continue until you hear that the prayers are coming to an end. Then ask the worship leader to sing the song once again.

2. He was intimate

Light a candle as a sign that God is present and ask each person to find a space where they can be intimate with God. Encourage them to kneel, lie prostrate or sit before God and pour out their heart of love for him. Ask them to write down their prayer of thanksgiving to God and explain to them that you want a couple of people at the end of this section to come and share what they have written. Encourage them to write a simple love song to God. Explain that it doesn't need to rhyme and they don't need to use flowery language. All they need to do is pour out their heart to God.

During this time either the worship band could continue to play or you could play a CD/cassette that has some appropriate music, preferably without words. After three or four minutes, ask a couple of people to come up and read their 'love songs' to God.

3. He prayed anywhere

Ask your group to go and visit the three prepared places in the venue, one at a time. Explain that there are three areas: one for their work or education life, one for their family life, and another for their social life. As they visit each place, they should write down on the piece of paper displayed there their commitment to bring God into decisions in that area of their lives. Encourage them to ask God to open their eyes and remind them to pray when they are busy and life seems to be full. Suggest they spend a few minutes praying at each place for that particular area of their life and for those who would interact with them before coming back to the main part of the venue.

4. He was specific

Ask people to get into pairs and think of people and situations they have prayed about this week. Get them to discuss with each other how they can be specific in their prayers, then bring to God those people or situations and pray, not just for a blessing, but for God to do specific things.

5. He was persistent

At this point bring to people's attention the poster at the front of the venue, which says 'Never give up!' Ask them to shout before God 'We will not give up! We will not lose heart!' as a declaration that they will not give up and they will be persistent in their prayers.

6. He prayed in faith

Ask the band to start to play 'The great awakening' again, or another suitable song. After playing the first verse and chorus they should keep the music playing and over the music ask the audience to cry out to God for a greater measure of faith. Ask them to speak out their prayers all together; to speak out their commitment to believe God

despite the circumstances. Even if it seems as if their neighbour, friend or family member will never become a
Christian, encourage them to speak out their faith in God to
change circumstances. After a few moments, encourage
people back into the song and sing the first verse and chorus
again.

7. *He prayed with others*

Ask people to get into groups of three or four and begin to
pray together for God to move in your nation, city, town,
area. Suggest they pray for those ruling the land, for those
controlling the finances of your nation/town, for the police,
for those working in education and so on. Leave them to
pray for about five to ten minutes.

8. *He submitted to his Father's will*

Ask people to kneel before God as a sign that they willingly
submit to his lordship over their lives, and pray out a prayer
for everyone present.

Finish by encouraging people to continue in their own
'prayer walk' and to pray as Jesus did.

Imagination and Faith

40 Soaring Above the Clouds

This idea is based on Isaiah 40:29–31 where it talks about us soaring on wings like eagles. Many times throughout our lives we do not 'soar' but are very heavy-laden with our problems and difficulties. Many years ago, Ray and I heard a sermon that has stuck in our minds about soaring above our problems and not being under our problems. Out of the memory of that sermon I recently wrote a meditation, which is designed to help people soar above their problems and keep their eyes on God. This idea is good to use in any situation where you know your group is preoccupied with stress or many cares.

THE PREPARATION

If you are able, arrange to have Isaiah 40:29–31 displayed on the overhead or video screen at the appropriate point in your presentation. If you do not have these facilities, read the verses out and have people look them up in their Bibles.

You will also find it helpful to use my *A God Encounter* CD. You could either use the music on track 8 and arrange for someone to read the meditation given below, or you could play track 3 which has the words on it.

If you choose to have someone read the meditation, use someone with a clear strong voice and make sure they rehearse it beforehand.

THE IDEA

Encourage people to use their imagination to see themselves soaring through their problems and difficulties into the freedom that God brings. Ask them to get into a comfortable position, either by sitting back in their chair, feet on the floor and hands by their side, or by lying flat on the floor.

Perhaps light a few candles or have dimmed lighting. Make the atmosphere conducive to peace and rest. Play the appropriate track from my CD and read the meditation below.

Soaring Above the Clouds

You may feel you are surrounded by problems or difficulties that seem immovable. If this is the case, then come with me, as we ask God to help us soar through our problems into his freedom. Let's encourage our souls to soar high.

The Bible says, 'Those who hope in the Lord will renew their strength. They will soar on wings like eagles; they will run and not grow weary, they will walk and not be faint.' God, if we ask him, will help us to soar high – to fly through our problems – as an eagle soars through the clouds to the blue sky beyond.

So . . . close your eyes. Take a deep breath and hold it for a second and then expel the air slowly. Breathe in again and then let it out slowly. As you do this, feel your body beginning to relax. Now begin to use your imagination. See yourself rise from the ground and begin to fly. At first it might seem a struggle as you push through the clouds and climb into the sky. Train your mind to relax and leave your problems and stresses behind you. As you continue to soar upwards 'see' yourself come through the clouds, into the blue sky beyond.

As you rise above the clouds, see yourself rise above your problems. Begin to fly just like an eagle. Enjoy the freedom soaring and diving brings. Feel the warmth of the sun on you

*as you dance with the wind. All the time you are soaring, God
if you trust him, will give you strength to overcome your difficulties and problems. Soar high – fly high – relax in his presence and know his peace.*

*Those who hope in the Lord will renew their strength. They
will soar on wings like eagles. They will run and not grow
weary. They will walk and not faint.*

Nancy Goudie Copyright © Engage/NGM 2002

Afterwards, read out Isaiah 40:29–31 and finish with a
prayer asking God to help us overcome our problems, difficulties and stresses so that we can soar above them with him.

41 Speaking the Word

In Nehemiah 8 there is an account of the Book of the Law (the Bible of the time) being read publicly from daybreak until noon. Later on in that same chapter we realise that in fact the Book of the Law was read to the people publicly every day. It is so important to have the word of God in us, and one of the ways to do this is to read it consistently. I encourage people to read the whole Bible and not just their favourite chapters over and over again. I personally have used a Bible reading planner since 1979 and have read through the Bible over and over again. The Bible is an amazing book. It is not a book you read once and think, 'Well, I know it now. I don't have to read it again.' It's a book that has gems on every page. It doesn't matter how many times you have read the Bible from cover to cover, each time you read it you still learn so much from God.

If we want to be people who are intimate with God and are used in strategic ways in the kingdom of God, we need to know the word of God. This idea encourages people to read and explore the Bible and therefore increases their faith in God.

THE PREPARATION

Arrange for Nehemiah 8:1–3 and Romans 12 to be shown on the overhead or video screen at the appropriate times. Alternatively, ask people to bring a Bible with them.

Have some paper and pens in case people come without them. It would be handy to have extra Bibles too, should people need them.

Arrange for someone who has a good clear voice to read Romans 12. Have the following Bible study on Romans 12 printed on paper ready for distribution.

Romans 12

Discuss the following questions together and write down your conclusions.

1. Who wrote Romans?
2. When was it written?
3. Where was it written?
4. To whom was it written?
5. Read verse 1. What does it mean to offer your body as a living sacrifice?
6. Read verse 2. How can we renew our minds practically?
7. How do we discern God's will according to this chapter?
8. Verse 3 says we should have a sober judgement of ourselves. Normally we either think of ourselves too highly, or we think we're not capable of anything at all. We all fall into one of these categories more than the other. Which one do you naturally fall into and why? What can we do to have a sober judgement of ourselves?
9. Verse 9 says, 'Love must be sincere.' Look up 1 Corinthians 13 and list all the things that love should be, e.g. patient.
10. Read verse 10. How, practically, do we 'honour' others above ourselves?
11. Verse 13 commands us to practise hospitality. How can we do this in our everyday lives, especially if we don't have our own home?
12. Be honest! How easy/hard do you find verse 14? Where in Scripture does Jesus tell us we are blessed when people persecute us?

13. Read verse 19. What does this verse mean? Can you think of an example of this in the Bible?
14. Read verse 20. What does it mean to 'heap burning coals on his head'?

Read the instructions below on how to paraphrase, and display Romans 8:1 and my paraphrase on the overhead or video screen at the appropriate time. Alternatively, ask people to look it up in their Bible and read out my paraphrase.

Also read the instructions in Idea 31 on how to memorise so that you are confident of leading others in this exercise.

THE IDEA

Read Nehemiah 8:1–3 to your group. Explain to them that although you are not going to read the Bible for several hours, you *are* going to explore the Bible creatively together and ask God to speak to you through it.

Ask everyone to look up Romans 12 in their Bible, then have someone read the whole chapter. Afterwards read the chapter together out loud.

Hand out the Bible study notes and ask people to get into groups of four and complete the questions on Romans 12 together. You will need to give them around thirty to forty-five minutes to complete this. At the end of the Bible study ask for one representative from each group to read out their answers.

Once this has been done, ask them to stay in their groups and paraphrase the first eight verses of this chapter, with each person paraphrasing two verses. Explain that a para-phrase is not a direct translation, but it is someone using their own words to describe the meaning of the verse or verses. To help them understand, you could show the follow-ing verse from Romans 8:1: 'Therefore, there is now no condemnation for those who are in Christ Jesus', followed by my paraphrase 'Because of all that Jesus has done for us and because we know him as a friend, we do not need to live in guilt and shame.'

You will need to allow around ten minutes for this exercise. Once completed, ask each group (or if there are too many groups, choose three or four groups) to come and give their paraphrase of the first eight verses publicly.

If you still have time left, you could ask everyone to memorise Romans 12:12. Show them how to memorise by splitting the verse into three sections and memorising the first section until they think they can say it without looking at it and then proceed to memorising the first and second sections together and so on until they feel they know the three sections. Give them about five to ten minutes to do this. Ask several people to stand and say the verse and its Scripture reference publicly.

End by encouraging people to read the Bible more often. Have some Bible planners to give away or to sell, and challenge people to read through the whole Bible in a year or two (see Recommended Resources for details).

42 One Nation Under One King

We used this idea just recently at a conference called Emerge in Germany. At the conference we had around 1,200 people attend, with over twenty nations represented. We wanted to show that even though we came from different nations around the world, we were united together under one King. We brought huge logs from Britain and gave each country represented one log each. (You should have seen the looks we got as we transported many huge logs all the way from Britain to Germany. I am sure people would have been even more surprised had we told them what we were going to do with them!)

We asked each person with a log to bring it to the middle of the room and we bound the logs together with tape to show that the many logs had become one in Jesus. No longer were there any divisions. We committed ourselves to working together for God and his kingdom. It was a very exciting and strategic time.

THE PREPARATION

You will need to purchase or find the number of logs or sticks you require. We got ours from a garden centre locally.

If you are able, display Ezekiel 37:15–28 on the overhead or video screen as a person with a good clear voice reads that portion of Scripture. If you do not have overhead or video facilities, ask people to follow the verses in their Bibles.

You will need a strong marker pen and also some thick sticky binding tape and/or string.

THE IDEA

This idea is based on Ezekiel 37:15–28 which talks about unity and how God blesses unity. God tells the prophet Ezekiel to take a stick of wood and write on it 'Judah's stick' and then to take another stick and write on that 'Ephraim's stick'. He then tells Ezekiel to join the two sticks together and when his countrymen ask what it means he is to tell them that the two sticks will become one in God's hand. The whole chapter then goes on to say what God will do when the two sticks become one and how he will pour out his blessings upon them.

You can use this idea in several ways. One way would be when you have many churches in your town or area coming together for an event or service. You could use this idea when all your home groups come together as one, or you could use it with one home group, giving each person a stick. This symbolic gesture is represented in Psalm 133 where it says, 'How good and pleasant it is when brothers live together in unity . . . For there the Lord bestows his blessing' (verses 1, 3).

Give each person or group a stick and ask them to write their name on it or the name of the group or church. Have Ezekiel 37:15–28 read out and explain to people what you are about to do. Draw their attention to Psalm 133 and to the fact that God blesses unity. Remind them that God says in Ezekiel 37:26 that he will make a covenant of peace when there is unity and that he will increase our numbers and we will see so many more people come to know Jesus. Encourage them in the fact that as we draw together in unity and have a desire to move together for God and his kingdom, God will put his sanctuary among us and his dwelling place will be there (verses 26–27).

When everyone is clear on what you are about to do, ask those with the sticks to bring them into the middle and arrange for someone to bind all the sticks together with sticky tape or string. As they do so, verses 17–19 should be read out. After they are bound together, ask people to prophesy and pray out what the scriptures say will happen:

- No more division.
- Abundant blessings.
- Cleansing from God.
- Possession of the land.
- The generations being blessed.
- An everlasting covenant of peace.
- An increase in numbers of people being saved.
- God's presence in your town, area, church or group.
- God's sanctuary among his people.
- A testimony to the nations of the world.
- One nation under one King.

You can either have one person reading out the blessings one by one, asking your group to pray out loud together for that particular blessing to come into being, or you can ask individuals to pray and prophesy one blessing each until all the scriptures have been prayed. Go on – have some holy chaos and achieve some amazing things in God!

43 Reflections of the Father

As Christians we so often take the cross of Jesus for granted. We have grown up with the story that Jesus died for us and because it is so familiar the reality of it does not seem to touch us as it should. Because the cross is so central to our faith, it is important to bring home its truths in as many creative ways as we can. This monologue/meditation looks at the cross of Jesus from Father God's perspective. You will find that not only will this idea be relevant to Christians, but it will also present the cross to those who don't yet know Jesus in a real way.

THE PREPARATION

Ask someone to read the following monologue/meditation using track 6 of *Journey to the Cross* as background music. Do make sure you use someone who has a good clear voice and ask them to rehearse it beforehand with the backing track. Alternatively, you could play track 1 of *Journey to the Cross*, which has the music and the words.

THE IDEA

As part of your service or event, use the following monologue/meditation to bring home the reality of the cross. Ask people to sit in a comfortable position, with their eyes closed. Explain to them that this is a look at the cross of Jesus from Father God's perspective. It may be good to dim the lights at this point.

Relections of the Father

My heart leaps for joy as I remember the good times we've had since the beginning of time. With joy we danced as we lovingly formed our creation. With love we planned and shaped all things. It is with deep sadness that I remember when it all began to go wrong. Our creation turned against its creator, yet, my Son, we gently and carefully planned all that we could do in order to restore all things.

It was with sheer delight that I placed you in the womb of a woman and with joy and pride I watched you grow and develop into a man. Sometimes my heart overflowed with love and it spilled out as my words echoed throughout heaven and earth: 'This is my much loved Son – I take great delight in him.'

I watched with joy as our plan took shape and heaven was released on earth through you. When you touched people's hearts, when you touched diseased bodies, when you gave people faith and life, my heart was filled with hope.

It was with sadness that I saw the hatred in men's hearts towards you. How can they hate that which is good? My heart was filled with pain when I saw what they did to you as they spat upon you and beat your face with their fists. My heart burst when I saw them thrust a crown of thorns onto your head and whip your back until it looked deformed. I wanted to shout in your defence – I wanted to destroy all who so hurt you – yet I remembered our plan, my Son. You kept your side – I must keep mine.

It was with anger that I saw the forces of evil gathering to make their plans to destroy you. It was as though a sword went through my heart when they put the nails through your hands and feet. How could they do that to the Son I loved? As you hung on the cross, my Son, in sheer agony, I did my part, and with tears running down my face I blamed you, my much loved Son, for all the wrongs ever committed by our creation. With great emotion, I released my judgement, my anger, upon you and you paid the penalty for every sin ever committed. The pain was so huge, my Son, that I could not bear to look from heaven. I had to turn my aching heart away. The sun refused to shine, as nature realised what man had done. The angels stood amazed and shocked that I did not intervene, yet love for you kept the judgement coming 'til you bore every little part! I knew the end was near, but it was only the end of the beginning.

With sheer joy we danced again when we were reunited. We had done it. We had accomplished all of our plan. You had died but I raised you back to life, and in that moment I declared that you had conquered sin, death and hell. We rejoiced when we saw that through your life, death and resurrection many were discerning new life : freedom from fear and guilt, knowing for-giveness and discovering a relationship with us that will never ever fade away.

Nancy Goudie Copyright 1999 Engage/SGO 1999

At the end, ask people to get into pairs and share what they received from that meditation and pray for one another, or ask them to respond to God to become Christians or to give themselves afresh to God.

44 An Encounter – Face to Face

THE PREPARATION

Ask someone to read the following meditation. Choose someone with a good clear voice, who can use their imagination to 'see' what they are reading. You can use the backing track on *A God Encounter* (track 6) or alternatively you can play track 1 which has the words and the music.

THE IDEA

This meditation is a great tool to use to bring people right into the presence of God. You can use it during the worship time or as part of the talk. It is ideal if you are speaking on intimacy with God, perhaps using the story of the transfiguration. I have found that this meditation can open people's eyes to 'see' and discover Jesus as never before.

Face to Face

I want you to come with me on a journey – a journey that will take you face to face with Jesus and deep into the presence of God. When Moses met the Lord on the top of the mountain, he was a changed man. His whole appearance changed – he was never the same again. When Jesus took his disciples up to a high mountain, it was an experience never to be forgotten. If you come with me today, I will take you up the mountain of God to meet Jesus face to face – and if you truly meet God you will never be the same again, and it will be an experience you will never forget.

Close your eyes and use your imagination to see yourself at the top of a mountain. All around you are the wonders of God's creation: the beauty of the mountain ranges, the lakes beneath, the rivers running and dancing through the green grass. As you take in this magnificent scene, you are aware of the presence of the creator God all around you. Suddenly, before your eyes you see a door standing open in heaven and you are able to see into the holy of holies. It's as if a new dimension opens up to you. See yourself walking through the door onto the streets of pure gold. In front of you you see a sparkling river, shimmering like glass and flowing into a sea of pure crystal. As you take in this awesome sight you hear a voice calling your name. You turn and see the one who sits on the throne: the creator of the universe, the only true God, the King of kings and Lord of lords, the alpha and the omega, the beginning and the end. His face is shining; his clothes are dazzling white and blazed with light. You are blinded by the sheer brightness of his appearance. You fall to your knees and worship him. A cloud from heaven seems to descend upon you. The whole mountain seems to tremble – the glory of the Lord is all around. From within the cloud comes a voice: 'This is my Son, my chosen one. Listen to him.'

In the quietness open your ears to the voice of God. Hear what he has to say.

'My child, you are more precious to me than silver or gold, my heart aches for you, my Son died for you. Come close to me – hold tight to me. Let me wash you white as snow, let me heal you from within. I have come to bring you life and to bring you freedom. For, my child, I love you.'

Lord, thank you for your love and peace. Thank you for the freedom you bring into our lives. Thank you for taking us up your holy mountain. Help us, day by day, to take your love, your presence, your freedom to a hurting, needy world.

You may wish to have a response after this meditation. You can invite people to indicate that they wish to be prayed for, whether to give their lives to Jesus for the first time or whether to come back to God. You may also wish to get people into pairs to pray for each other after this meditation.

45 Dressed and Ready

I was in South Africa when I first saw this idea in action. A friend of ours introduced it while leading worship in his church. It captured our imagination so much that when Ray and I came back home to Britain, we started using it in our Heartbeat-led worship events. The idea is lots of fun, but it also helps to put God's word firmly in our minds.

THE PREPARATION

You will need to have read through Ephesians 6:10–18 and perhaps arrange for these verses to be displayed on the overhead or video screen.

THE IDEA

Arrange for all or part of your worship/talk to be on Ephesians 6:10–18, which tells us about the armour of God. At an appropriate place in your meeting, ask people to get into pairs with people of the same sex. Inform them that you are going to dress one another in the armour of God. Read from Ephesians 6:10–14. When you get to the belt of truth, ask them to put the imaginary belt of truth around their partner's waist. The first person does it to their partner, then vice versa. Once they have done this, go on to the breastplate of righteousness and ask them to put it on and pretend to tie it up at the back. Ask them to place on their partner's feet the shoes of the gospel of peace, then the shield of faith and finally the helmet of salvation.

At the end, tell them they are clothed and ready for battle. Point out that God did not give us any protection for our back. The Bible says we are not to be people who give up and turn back but those who press on and win through.

If appropriate, you can then move into a time of prayer/intercession.

46 Prayer in All Directions

I have used this idea many times in my Spiritual Health Weekends because it is a great way of encouraging people to pray publicly without having the pressure of hearing their own voice. It is also a good way of encouraging prayer, even when you don't have a lot of time available.

THE PREPARATION

If you are using this idea with a large audience, make sure you have a P.A. set up, as you will need it.

THE IDEA

Ask everyone to stand, and explain to them that you are going to lead them in a time of prayer. Say that you are going to pray in four directions – to the north, south, east and west – and ask them to face the back of the hall. Ask them to imagine they are in their own home facing north. If they do not know where the north is they should pick one direction (it does not really matter). Ask them to see in their mind's eye what lies in that direction. Is it schools, neighbours, friends, family, council buildings, town or city? Whatever lies in that direction they should pray for those people – that God would impact them with the power of his Spirit and that revival would come to that place. Ask them to speak out their prayers until you give the word to turn to another direction. Encourage them to pray out loud and not to worry about what others are thinking, because they will not hear what they are saying as each person will be praying out loud.

After a number of minutes in one direction, ask everyone to turn to the right and pray to the 'east'. Again, get them to imagine all that lies in that direction and encourage them to pray for God to move. Do the same for the 'south' and the 'west'. End with a prayer from the front, thanking God for all he has done and is going to do through the prayers that have been said. Perhaps end this section of your meeting by asking everyone to shout, 'Let it be so.'

Using All Senses

47 Communion of the Senses – Version 1

I have used this idea, or a version of it, over the last six years at each of my Spiritual Health weekends at the beginning of January. I, and many of the people who attend the conferences, have found this communion service to be an intimate time with Jesus. It can change people's lives in such a way that they are never the same again. My prayer is that as you use this idea in your church or event God will move in a powerful way and bring each of you into a new experience of who he is.

THE PREPARATION

Prepare the communion table by displaying lots of different kinds of bread. Get a selection from your local supermarket, looking for those that will stimulate the taste buds and arouse the senses. Make sure you buy bread that is fresh that morning because the smell of the freshly cooked bread will add to the service. Buy a good quality wine and open the bottles before the service begins. Provide a nice non-alcoholic drink (perhaps red grape juice) for those who cannot take wine. Display the bread and wine on a table at a prominent place at the front of the church or room. If wished, place in between the bread small nite-light candles, and make sure you light them just before the service begins.

   If you can, prepare and display the songs, prayers, verses, etc. on the overhead or video screen at the appropriate place (see the programme for details). If you do not have overhead or video facilities, have the information on printed sheets or ask people beforehand to bring their Bibles.

You will need someone to read the meditation given below. Ask someone who has a good clear voice and make sure they rehearse with a backing track beforehand. I would suggest you use track 6 of *Journey to the Cross*.

THE IDEA

Announce to the group that you are going to celebrate communion together. Ask if anyone knows the meaning of the word 'communion'. Display the following on the overhead or video screen and explain that this is the dictionary definition of the word 'communion'.

COMMUNION – The sharing of thoughts and feelings. Intimacy at the highest level. Fellowship and friendship.

Encourage the group that you are going to experience a deeper intimacy with God through this communion service. Throughout the service you are going to use all your senses of touch, taste, smell, sight and hearing. Go through each sense with everyone. Use your prepared overhead or video to display the following or hand out the prepared printed paper:

TASTE   *Psalm 34:8*
          'Taste *and see that the Lord is good; blessed is the man who takes refuge in him.*'
SMELL   *2 Corinthians 2:15–16*
          '*For we are to God the* aroma *of Christ among those who are being saved and those who are perishing. To the one we are the* smell *of death; to the other, the* fragrance *of life.*'

SIGHT   Isaiah 6:1
               'In the year that King Uzziah died, I saw the
               Lord seated on a throne, high and exalted, and
               the train of his robe filled the temple.'
HEARING   Galatians 3:2
               'I would like to learn just one thing from you: Did
               you receive the Spirit by observing the law, or by
               believing what you heard?'
TOUCH   Luke 24:39
               'Look at my hands and my feet. It is I myself!
               Touch me and see; a ghost does not have flesh
               and bones, as you see I have.'

Give an illustration of intimacy. For example, ask people to
get into pairs and imagine that one of them is blind. When
you are introduced to someone you would observe their face
and what they look like, but when a blind person is introduced to someone they cannot know what that person is like
unless they ask if they can feel their face with their hands.
Ask the person who is pretending to be blind to examine the
face of their partner. You will find that people will be very
embarrassed at the thought of doing this, but once the 'buzz'
of excitement and embarrassment has died down, explain
that the reason why the whole procedure is embarrassing is
because to touch someone's face like that can be very intimate. Explain that Jesus wants us to come so close to him
that it's as if we were touching him.

   Prepare people for communion by asking them to close
their eyes and concentrate on the words spoken through this
meditation. Ask them to imagine they are the person being
spoken about in the meditation.

Crucified

The last few years with Jesus have just been tremendous. You have come to love and believe in him. You have seen him do incredible miracles in front of your eyes and the wisdom coming from him is amazing. He seems to know the right thing to say in each situation. He makes you feel important and deeply loved. No one has loved you the way Jesus has. He has become a special friend. Surely he must be the Messiah, the one you've been waiting for. However, this morning you have heard news that must be wrong. Someone came to your door and told you that Jesus was arrested last night and that the authorities were going to kill him today. Fear and panic rise in your being. Jesus has had death threats before – surely he will just walk away from this as he has done in the past?

You begin to calm down. Jesus will do something, surely! You decide to go and see for yourself. Out in the street, everyone is talking about Jesus being arrested. You overhear snippets of conversation about him being taken to Golgotha (the Place of the Skull where they often crucify people). You run outside the city and there you meet up with the others who cared and provided for Jesus, and as you look Jesus is being laid on a cross. Everything within you screams 'NO!' as you hear the hammer knocking the nails into his hands and feet. There are many throwing insults at Jesus, mocking him, and you want to stop them, but fear and bewilderment hold you back. 'What's going on, Jesus? What's happening? What about all the plans we had for the future? You are the Messiah. Come down from the cross – show them who you really are.' But Jesus stays there, hanging, dying.

Darkness covers the whole land. The sun disappears as though it does not want to shine on a day like today. The women around you are weeping; the disciples, Jesus' close friends, are all confused. This cannot be happening. Suddenly,

Jesus calls out, 'Father, into your hands I commit my Spirit.'

It's all over. He's dead! The friend you loved and trusted has gone. Confusion and fear are raging within you. You wait with the others until the body of Jesus is taken down from the cross. You follow them and see them placing the body into a tomb. Together with some women you decide to visit his tomb to anoint his body with spices after the Sabbath.

Very early on the first day of the week, you meet together and hurry towards the tomb. You talk about how you are going to remove the huge stone which they have rolled across the entrance. However, when you reach the tomb, you notice that the stone has already been rolled away and the guards who are supposed to be watching the tomb have disappeared. What's happened? You walk into the tomb and see a young man sitting there in a white robe, who tells you that Jesus is alive. JESUS IS ALIVE!? What does he mean? How can he be? You are bewildered and you notice that your hands are trembling. You start to run to tell his disciples, but someone stands in front of you. You look up and there standing in front of you is Jesus. Joy and excitement suddenly fill your being as you exclaim, 'You're alive, you're alive!' You fall to the ground and worship him. Jesus – you're alive!

Nancy Goudie Copyright © Engage 1995

At the end of the meditation, ask someone to sing an appropriate song. My suggestion would be 'Amazing grace', 'When I survey' or 'Thorns' (details of this in Resources), but feel free to pick whatever song you think would be appropriate. It is better to ask one person to sing rather than the whole group, as often people can be quite emotional after this meditation. Alternatively, you could play a recording of an appropriate song.

Have someone read the following communion song next.

Communion Song of the Five Senses

Red from the blood shed freely for us,
Colour of kings in royal array.
Blood from the King of kings – for all time,
We remember with bread and wine.

Wholesome the scent of freshly made bread,
Speaking of life that was broken and shared.
Perfume of this dear sacrifice,
We remember with bread and wine.

Rich in the taste of wine on the tongue,
Reaching our hearts with the love of the Son.
Savouring bread, we think of his death,
We remember with bread and wine.

Soft is the bread, smooth is the wine,
Gentle this touch in the hearts that are yours.
We feel you near, around and within,
You have washed us with bread and wine.

Wonderful living words we can hear,
Reading the Scriptures with listening ears.
Worshipping him, so great and divine,
We remember with bread and wine.

Red is the colour, and rich is the taste,
Wholesome the smell, and soft is the bread,
Holy the words we utter each time
We remember with bread and wine.

Helen Graham. Used with permission

At this point pray, or ask someone to, thanking God for the bread and wine, which speak so clearly to us of all Jesus accomplished at the cross. Then encourage people to go to the table and take a piece of bread. Explain to them that there are lots of different types of bread and they should take time in choosing which bread they would like.

Ask them to use their senses as they take the bread. They should *look* at the bread, *smell* the bread, *touch* the bread, *taste* the bread and ask God to *speak* to them through the bread. Tell them that as they smell the bread it may make them feel hunger – there is nothing like the aroma of freshly baked bread to stimulate the taste buds. Each person should pray individually, asking God to increase their hunger for him. The bread may speak to them of life or fullness, therefore encourage them to pray for a deeper walk with God; that he would fill them with the fullness of his life.

When it comes to the wine, remind people to again use their senses. *Look* at the wine, *smell* it before *tasting* it. As you look at the wine and smell it, it may speak to you about richness and quality. Encourage everyone to pray for a richer, deeper and more quality intimacy with God. Again remind everyone to keep their ears open to the voice of God as he may speak to them through the wine.

During this time play appropriate background music. It is often better to use a CD or cassette to enable the worship leaders to enter into the whole experience of communion. (For suggested music see the Resources.) However, perhaps towards the end of the prayer time, you could ask the worship leader to lead people in an appropriate worship song.

After communion, ask everyone to join you in expressing the following vow to God as a declaration that because of all Jesus has done at the cross they will serve him and follow him to the end. At the end encourage everyone to shout their praises to God.

Communion Vow

Lord, we stand together as a company of your people to dedicate ourselves to you and your kingdom. We recognise that the battle is hard and that the stakes are high, but no matter what lies ahead, how difficult, tough or hard the battle may be, we dedicate ourselves to you, our King. We will stand and fight with you and will not be like those who shrink back from the battle and are destroyed, but will be of those who believe, who are bold and who are courageous. Thank you that through your cross we have the victory. Yes! Yes! Yes!

© Nancy Goudie 2002

48   Communion of the Senses – Version 2

THE PREPARATION

For the preparation, see Version 1 of this idea (Idea 47). Use track 5 of *Journey to the Cross* for the meditation, or pick someone with a good clear voice to read out the meditation (given below), using track 10 of the same CD/cassette as background music.

THE IDEA

Use the same introduction as Version 1, again giving the dictionary definition of the word 'communion'. State that God is inviting people to an intimate supper with him. Remind them that 2,000 years ago Jesus met with his friends for an intimate supper in an upper room. Exhort them to listen to God's invitation to us to 'come and eat' with him.

Read the following, which is my paraphrase of Isaiah 55:1–3.

Isaiah 55 – God's Invitation to Us

Come, all of you who are thirsty. Come to me and drink.
Come, all of you who are weak and heavy-laden. I will give you
  rest.
Come, all of you who are hungry, and I will fill you with bread
  from heaven.
Come, all of you who have no money, no resources. Come buy
  and eat.

169

Come drink of my wine without money and without cost.
Don't worry if you have no money. What I want to give you is
    priceless – money couldn't purchase it.
Come, come eat of my bread.
Why sell your soul for bread that is not from heaven?
Why strive for wine that does not satisfy?
Listen, listen to me and come and eat with me.
Give ear, listen to me and hear what is good for your soul.
I have made an everlasting covenant with you.
My promises and my covenant will never fail.

Come, come and eat. Come, come and drink and be filled with
    the very breath of heaven.

Say to the group, 'We have heard the invitation to come and
sit in God's presence. Now let's respond to him by saying the
following together.'

Read the following prayer out loud with the congregation.

Our Response to God

Lord, we hear your invitation and we respond by saying, 'Lord,
    we will come.'
Lord, we come as a hungry and thirsty people to meet with you
    our living God.
We long to drink at your table, Lord . . . we long to eat of your
    bread of life.
Speak to us. Reveal yourself to us. Take us deeper than we have
    ever gone before. We are hungry for you. Amen.

Read Mark 15:16–20, 22–30, 33–39. Then invite people to
close their eyes as they are led through a meditation of the
cross. Explain that they are about to be taken on a journey
back 2,000 years to see the cross of Calvary from what could

have been Barabbas's viewpoint. Encourage them to imagine
that the person in the meditation is themselves.

It Should Have Been Me

*In this meditation, I want you to imagine you are a Jew living
2000 years ago when Israel was conquered by the Romans.*

*Close your eyes and use your imagination to see yourself in
a dungeon. You are a prisoner and you only have a few hours
left to live before the authorities are going to crucify you. All
sorts of regrets fill your mind: Why did I fight? Why did I
murder that man? You try to put your thoughts aside, but the
anticipation of death ahead seems to cloud and darken your
mind. Nothing seems to take away the agony and utter devas-
tation you feel. You joke with the others in your cell that today
is your big day, but everything within you is screaming for a way
out. You wonder how you are going to face your family and
friends. You begin to pray for a brave heart but end up screaming inwardly for God to forgive you and get you out of this mess.
Heaven seems to be closed to you and you decide if there really
is a God then either he is sleeping or he doesn't hear prayers
from a waster like you. You feel as though your head is going
to explode with the heaviness of your thoughts, but at that
precise moment the door is opened and your jailer tells you it's
time for you to leave. You get up to walk out of your cell, but
your legs give way from under you. You stumble across the
room, knowing that this will be the last walk you will ever take.*

*As you reach the entrance to the cell you are told you are to
be taken to see the governor. You don't understand why, but
think this must be one of their 'procedures' before your ulti-
mate journey's end – dying on a rough tree they call a 'cross'.*

*Your heart is beating wildly as you walk into the governor's
room. He takes one look at you and says, 'You are free to go!'*

*'Free to go? What do you mean? How can this be? I am due
to be crucified today!'*

The governor's reply seems to echo throughout the prison: 'You are free because someone else took your place. He was crucified instead of you.'

You can hardly take the words in! Your heart is thumping in your chest – so many questions fill your mind: Why did someone else die in my place? Why am I being given the right to live? Relief floods through your whole being. You are alive, you are no longer condemned to die, all your guilt has been cancelled out, you are free.

You quickly leave the prison and run into the fresh air. You look at the grass, the trees, the leaves, the sky. Thankfulness and joy floods your being as you fill your lungs with fresh pure air. On the horizon across the sky you suddenly see three crosses. You run out of the city to the hill called Golgotha and there in the middle of two thieves is the man who took your place. Above his torn and bruised body is the inscription 'Jesus – the king of the Jews'. You look at his bloodied feet and hands where crude metal has brutally nailed them to the tree. You see his back where it looks as though he's been whipped dozens of times until his back is like a ploughed field. You look at his head – pierced with thorns until the blood is constantly running down his face. You look into his eyes, and inwardly you gasp because you are surprised at what you see. Instead of fear and anger you see love and forgiveness. He looks straight at you and seems to know who you are. In the depth of his pain he seems to smile and say, 'It's OK. It's OK.' You turn away and with tears in your eyes, you shout to the skies, 'God, it should have been me! It should have been me! This man has done nothing. It should have been me!'

At the end of the meditation, tell the group that in fact it should have been us who died on that cross 2,000 years ago, but Jesus died instead of us. He gave everything for us, so let's give all we have for him. But let's also remember that 2,000 years ago the story did not end at the cross. Three days later Jesus arose from the dead, victorious over sin, death and hell.

Next, read the communion song given in Idea 47, and then pray, thanking God for Jesus and for all that was accomplished at the cross. Thank him for the symbols we have of the bread and the wine, and ask him to make himself more real to you as you worship at his feet and eat the bread and drink the wine.

Encourage people to come forward for the bread and the wine, using all their senses, as described in Idea 47.

After communion get into groups of two or three to pray for one another. Then ask the worship leaders to lead you in a time of worship to God.

At the very end of the service encourage people to say the following communion vow as a declaration of their love and devotion to our amazing God. At the end encourage everyone to shout the words YES! YES! YES!

Communion Vow

Lord, we stand here today to declare that we are your people. We declare we will chase after you, God. We will pursue you with all of our heart because we know that if we do so we will be found by you. Thank you that in your word you call us a chosen people, indeed a holy people, a people belonging to you.

Lord, we push aside all that hinders our walk with you, we cast aside all obstacles, trample over all that would hold us back, because we are determined to put our faith and trust in you. No matter what we go through in life, whether heartaches, fears, discouragements or disappointments, we are determined to go on trusting you. We know, Lord, that as we stand and trust you we will never be put to shame. You will always deliver us.

Thank you, God, that you love us with an everlasting love – a love which is stronger and deeper than any human love. Thank you that on the cross of Calvary you demonstrated your unique love towards us.

Thank you that through your victory on the cross we can have victory in our lives. We declare that we will stand and serve you, our amazing God.

YES! YES! YES!

© Nancy Goudie 2002

49 Prayer Tunnel – Version 1

This is an idea that I saw in action for the first time at an evangelists' conference in England. The speaker at the meeting was Ed Silvoso and he had suggested to those of us who were on the committee that he would like to pray for people at the end using a prayer tunnel. Through this idea God moved in an enormously powerful way. It was as though heaven had come to earth that night.

The main part of the meeting had finished at approximately 8.30 pm and then we moved on to praying people through the tunnel. The next time I looked at the clock I was shocked to discover it was after midnight. The meeting finished at around 2.30 am. God had moved powerfully on so many people's lives. A glimpse of revival touched that meeting and many people's lives will never be the same again. This was an event that people have talked about for years.

A week or so later, I introduced the idea of a prayer tunnel to one of our NGM meetings, with similar results. God moved in such a special way we saw glimpses of heaven on earth. I also used it a month or so later at my Spiritual Health Weekend and again God visited us with his grace. Many were in tears as God moved in their lives in a powerful way.

Since that time I have adapted what I experienced at the evangelists' conference and the following two ideas came into being.

THE PREPARATION

You will need at least ten people who are willing to pray for others. Ask those who you know have a strong heart for prayer and who are preferably in some form of church leadership. You will also need a small bottle of oil for anointing. Choose a nice-smelling oil – perhaps of frankincense or myrrh (the incense given to Jesus at his birth) – which will stay with the person for some time. If you have a large group of 100 or more, have two tunnels comprising at least ten people each. If you are using this idea in a cell or small group, have a small tunnel appropriate to the number of people.

You will need to show those who will be making the tunnel how and where they should stand. If you are having ten people in one tunnel, five people should stand in a straight line with the other five opposite them. I have always found it essential to rehearse this beforehand so that when the time comes it will happen quickly and efficiently. They should not hold hands or touch one another but face one another with enough room between them for someone to walk through. Explain to those you have chosen to pray that as a person walks through the tunnel, they should spend a few minutes praying for that person, asking God to bless them, laying hands on them and praying over them. Encourage your pray-ers to pray for the person and their family, praying out anything they receive prophetically, as long as it will encourage, build up and comfort. Explain that they will only have two or three minutes on each person and that the people going through the line need to keep on walking to the next couple after a few minutes at the most.

Pick one person to be at the beginning of the tunnel to anoint each person with the oil. They should pray that each person would meet with Jesus in a deep way as they walk through the tunnel.

Arrange for your musicians and/or worship leader to be ready to lead people in worship during the time that everyone is being prayed for. Do warn them that it may take quite some time for everyone to be prayed for, so they need to have thought this through previously. You could also use taped worship music, but do look to see what songs are on the CDs and cassettes beforehand to check whether they are appropriate for your meeting.

THE IDEA

At the end of the talk, or at a suitable part of your programme, explain to people that you would like each person to be prayed for individually, but rather than doing this the normal way, you are going to arrange for each person to be prayed for individually by at least ten people.

Ask your prearranged prayer people to form a tunnel or tunnels while the musicians lead the audience in worship to God. Encourage people to come forward row by row to be prayed for. Make sure the person who has the anointing oil is ready to pray for each person as they come forward to go through the tunnel. Make sure people go through the tunnel one by one.

My prayer is that as each person is prayed for again and again, God will meet with them in such a deep way that they will never be the same again.

50   Prayer Tunnel – Version 2

A couple of years after I saw God use the prayer tunnel to
bring people into a deeper walk with him, I decided to use
the idea again at my Spiritual Health Weekends, but this
time I felt I should ask the people forming the prayer tunnel
to pray for each individual's senses as they walked through.
Again as people went through the tunnel God moved in
incredible ways and powerful things happened not only to
those who walked through, but also to their families who
were not even at the conference.

THE PREPARATION

You will need at least twelve people to form the tunnel: one
couple to pray for each of the five senses, plus another
couple to pray for the sense organ of the mind – the imagination or, in other words, faith. Again ask those who you
know have a strong heart for prayer and choose those who
are preferably in some form of church leadership. Show
them how and where they should stand, as described in Idea
49, and give each couple a sense to pray for. For example, the
first couple could pray for hearing; that God would open up
the person's ears to hear what he is saying to them, and that
their intimacy with God would increase so that they hear his
voice more clearly than ever before.

Make sure each couple has a different sense to pray for –
hearing; sight; touch; taste; smell; imagination/faith and
explain the procedure given in Idea 49.

Again, arrange for your musicians to lead people in

worship for quite a length of time, or choose an appropriate CD/cassette.

THE IDEA

At the end of the talk, or at a suitable part of your programme, explain to people that they are going to be prayed for individually, with the pray-ers concentrating on each of the following senses.

Sight

That their spiritual eyes would be opened; that they would have a greater insight into what God is doing and how it affects society; that they would begin to see more clearly what God would want them to do.

Hearing

That God would open their ears to hear what he is saying; that greater intimacy would be the order of the day in their relationship with Christ. So many people find it difficult to hear from God, so pray-ers would pray that their spiritual ears would be open to the voice of God.

Touch

That they would be touched by the living Lord and that his touch would affect their heart and emotions in a deep way. One touch from God could radically alter the whole of their lives.

Taste

That God would help them to 'taste and see that he is good'; that they would be able not only to 'hear' what God has for them, but experience it in everyday life.

Smell

That their lives would smell of the very presence of God;
that no matter where they go, those they meet would know
that they are in touch with the living God; that the fragrance
of God in them would impact lives everywhere.

Imagination/faith

That God would move in their imagination in order that they
would be able to believe him for more; that they would see
with their imagination what God wants to do in them and
through them and that their faith would increase so that they
could believe for more than they have ever done before.

Ask your prearranged pray-ers to form a tunnel or tunnels
with six couples in each. While the musicians lead the group
in worship, encourage people to come forward row by row to
be prayed for. As they come out of the tunnel, get them to
write down what they felt God said to them during their
'prayer walk'. Make sure you tell them to test any prophetic
words with their spiritual leaders.

It may be good to have a book available where people can,
if they wish, record what God said or did during the
meeting. I have found this to be a very encouraging way of
finding out what went on in the meeting. Explain that they
can write anonymously and that you are only recording it so
that it can be a testimony to the grace of God. Again, my
prayer is that God will move in people's lives and stimulate
their senses to our amazing God.

Index of Themes

Locators refer to idea numbers and not page numbers

Index of Bible References

Recommended Music and Resources

CDS AND CASSETTES

Steve

Falling Down

'Steve' are a powerful four piece guitar band who have a real passion for God and a heart for worship. This is an album full of fresh, creative worship sounds. You can purchase this CD through www.shiftrecords. com or from Christian bookshops. Price £14.99

Suse

It is well

Suse has a powerful vocal delivery and exudes a deep heart for worship. Her delivery of the song 'Thorns' has brought many into a fresh experience of God. You can purchase this CDEP through www.ngm.org.uk or through NGM (address on page 189). Price £3.98

Andy Hunter

Exodus

Andy who is one of NGM's talented DJs, is a man marked out by his passion for Jesus. He has been working over the last number of years in the mainstream clubs as a DJ but has also been pioneering leading people in worship using the decks. You can purchase this CD through www.shiftrecords.com or www.andyhunter.com or through NGM or through any Christian bookshop.

Doug E. Ross

Existence

Doug is another of NGM's DJs and has a deep desire to see God move through the club culture. Doug's anointed worship music will inspire you to go deeper with God. You can purchase this CDEP through www.ngm.org.uk or www.dougeross.com or through NGM. Price £3.99

Nancy Goudie

Journey to the Cross

A powerful CD and cassette that will take you to the foot of the cross to experience Christ's death, and impact you with the amazing love of God. You can purchase this CD or cassette through www.nancygoudie.com or www.ngm.org.uk or through NGM (details overleaf). Price £9.99 and £6.99

A God Encounter

A unique meditative worship experience which will transport you to the very throne room of God. You can purchase this CD through www.nancygoudie.com or www.ngm.org.uk or through NGM. Price £9.99

Delirious

Glo

Delirious are well known throughout the world for their ability to lead people in worship. This inspiring album will help you go deeper into God's presence. You can purchase this CD through any Christian bookshop or through Furious?records, P.O. Box 40, Arundel BN18 0UQ.

OTHER PRODUCTS FROM NANCY GOUDIE

Nancy Goudie's Spiritual Health Workout

This unique book is practical, accessible and fun to use and will help you exercise your faith muscles and tone up your heart for God. Price £6.99 and published by Kingsway Publications. You can purchase this book at any Christian bookshop or through www.nancygoudie.com

Bible Reading Planners

A superb way of systematically reading through the Bible in a year or two years. You can purchase these through www.nancygoudie.com or www.ngm.org.uk or through NGM (details below). Priced 50p each

Dealing with Disappointment – video

Each one of us experiences disappointment, despair or discouragement at sometime in our lives. The key is how we deal with these issues when the wind of adversity blows. In this video, Nancy Goudie draws upon her many years of experience in full time ministry to bring a message of hope and joy to those dealing with disappointment. You can purchase this video through www.nancygoudie.com or www.ngm.org.uk or through NGM. Price £5.99

Nancy Goudie's Spiritual Health Weekends – teaching tapes

Experience Nancy's teaching at her Spiritual Health Weekends. For details contact www.nancygoudie.com or NGM. Price £3.00 per cassette.

NGM CONTACT DETAILS

NGM, Caedmon Complex, Bristol Road, Thornbury, Bristol BS35 3BA
Tel: 01454 414880/2 Fax: 01454 414812
Email: ngm@ngm.org.uk
Web: www.ngm.org.uk

NANCY GOUDIE CONTACT DETAILS

Please write care of NGM above or email:
nancy@nancygoudie.com
Web: www.nancygoudie.com

About the Author

Nancy Goudie, along with her husband Ray, has been in full-time Christian ministry since 1980. She became a Christian when, at the age of six, she had a very dramatic and powerful experience of God. During the first twenty-two years of her life, she attended a Brethren church in her home town of Ayr, Scotland. During her teens she became part of a well-established Christian band called Unity. As well as singing with the band, she put her qualifications in speech (ALCM) to good use by being one of the narrators in the musicals that Unity produced.

In 1981, Ray and Nancy founded and led the internation-ally known band Heartbeat. As one of the singers and main speakers, she travelled and ministered throughout the UK and abroad and saw many young people being touched by the power of God. Since Heartbeat's ministry finished in 1991, her gifts of preaching and teaching have been used not only in Britain but in mainland Europe and the USA. She has also been interviewed on radio and television numerous times about her faith in God and has a regular teaching spot on UCB radio.

Nancy has written three books, *Developing Spiritual Wholeness* (1992), *Nancy Goudie's Spiritual Health Plan* (1995) and *Nancy Goudie's Spiritual Health Workout* (2001), as well as writing many articles for magazines and newspapers. She has also recorded two powerful meditation CDs/cassettes through which many have come into a deeper and more intimate walk with Jesus.

Nancy and Ray have two sons, Daniel (14) and Aidan (5), and are the directors of the international pioneering youth ministry, NGM. Ray and Nancy left Scotland in 1980 with a vision from God to start a ministry through which God could reach the youth of their land. They now have over 100 people working full time with them in evangelism, church planting, the media and training, and have seen thousands of young people in Britain and abroad come into a vibrant living relationship with the Lord Jesus. Both individually and corporately they live by faith and have seen God provide for their ministry in miraculous ways over and over again. Last year they completed a huge walk of faith, having seen God release £3 million to purchase and build a Missions and Arts Centre in Thornbury, near Bristol, England where they are based.

To find out more about Nancy and the work she does, visit her website at www.nancygoudie.com. You can also find out more about NGM by visiting their website at www.ngm.org.uk

NANCY GOUDIE'S SPIRITUAL HEALTH WEEKENDS

THREE EXCITING DAYS TO TRANSFORM YOUR WALK WITH GOD

Would you like to be pampered physically and toned up spiritually?

Nancy Goudie's Spiritual Health Weekends could be just the thing you are looking for!

Nancy Goudie runs weekend conferences at the beginning of each year (January and February) at a luxury four-star Hilton Hotel in Bristol. The first two weekends are for ladies only, with the third weekend being for men and women. Come and enjoy the excellent food and leisure facilities (spa, steam room, sauna, fitness room and luxury pool) and also experience God through the inspirational teaching and creative spiritual exercises from Nancy. Special guests include some of the talented NGM artists. These weekend conferences are booked well in advance so please book early to avoid disappointment.

For more information and booking details contact:

Nancy Goudie at NGM, Caedmon Complex, Bristol Road, Thornbury, Bristol BS35 3JA.
Tel: 01454 414880/2; Fax: 01454 414812;
email: nancygoudie@ngm.org.uk
or visit the website on www.nancygoudie.com